The Blend

How to Successfully Manage a Career and a Family

Tobi Asare is a mum of two and the founder of My Bump Pay, an online platform giving women the tools to smash the glass ceiling when they have a baby on the way and beyond. After studying Law at the University of Manchester and the BPP Law School in London, Tobi spent over ten years working with talented entrepreneurs who've built seriously impressive businesses. As well as running My Bump Pay, Tobi is now a director and sits on the board of one of the UK's largest media companies, running the business development, marketing and PR division. She received an award from Prime Minister Boris Johnson for her work helping women in the workplace.

The Blend

How to Successfully Manage a Career and a Family

First published in 2023 by HEADLINE HOME
An imprint of HEADLINE PUBLISHING GROUP

1

Cataloguing in Publication Data is available from the British Library

Hardback ISBN 978 1 4722 9601 6
eISBN 978 1 4722 9603 0

Designed and Typeset by Avon DataSet Ltd, Alcester, Warwickshire

Printed and bound in Great Britain by Clays Ltd, Elcograf S.p.A.

Headline's policy is to use papers that are natural, renewable and
recyclable products and made from wood grown in sustainable forests.
The logging and manufacturing processes are expected to conform to the
environmental regulations of the country of origin.

HEADLINE PUBLISHING GROUP
An Hachette UK Company
Carmelite House
50 Victoria Embankment
London EC4Y 0DZ

www.headline.co.uk
www.hachette.co.uk

To my incredible parents, who have shown me
through deep love and sacrifice how to show up
for your family, navigate The Blend
and chase your dreams.

To my husband: thank you for your unwavering support.

To my children: the world is your oyster!

Contents

Introduction   1

Chapter 1: Starting a family   11

Chapter 2: All things money and babies   43

Chapter 3: Building a successful career during
            your pregnancy   75

Chapter 4: Planning a successful maternity leave   107

Chapter 5: Freelancers and founders – building a
            business and a family   133

Chapter 6: Childcare   161

Chapter 7: Nailing your return to work   181

Chapter 8: Confidence   223

Chapter 9: Beyond the return – navigating life as
            a working mum   247

Chapter 10: For the allies – how can we help working
            mums and mums-to-be thrive in the
            workplace?   283

Chapter 11: Finding your way to the top   293

Acknowledgements   317

Notes   319

Resources   325

Index   329

Introduction

This book is for anyone ambitious. It's for you if you are thinking about having a family at some point in your professional life. If you are a new mum. If you are already a mum and thinking about expanding your family. If you are a mum looking for inspiration as you navigate the working world, and are finding parts of it difficult. If you are thinking about what your professional life looks like beyond the early days of motherhood. If you had your kids years ago and want to continue to push ahead in your career. If you're wondering how to break the glass ceiling. It's for you if you are deciding between full-time employment and self-employment as a mum or mum-to-be. It's for you if you are in a position of influence where you work, or you manage people who will at some point have children of their own. While it is written from the perspective of a woman, I would be delighted if men would read it too, to build an appreciation of the journey that many working mothers find themselves on, and to take the opportunity to implement change where possible.

This book is the book I was so desperately searching for back in 2017. This is not just about making it work or staying sane; this is about how to thrive, and how to set yourself up for success before the baby comes along, during the pregnancy and beyond. I start at the very beginning of the journey, from the moment that you think you might want a child, and start to wonder how the hell you are going to make it work and still have a fulfilling and successful career, and take you right through to the point when you might be considering a second or third child. I also explore the journey of women who are flying high in the most senior positions you can find in industry. Within the pages of this book, you will find a combination of the facts (don't skip them, because they are really important), practical, real-life, tried-and-tested tips that work, my personal experiences, and the stories of inspiring women – and a very supportive dad – who share their words of wisdom regarding different stages of the journey. Everyone who has shared has done so as if they're passing down refreshingly honest nuggets of wisdom to a sister or a best friend, because we all need knowledge to guide and help us find our way on this journey. Many of the people who have shared their stories have played really important roles in my own life, or are incredible individuals whom I really admire, so I thought it would be a powerful thing to give their voices a platform to inspire and encourage as many people as possible.

The biggest takeaway of my working motherhood journey is that there is no such thing as balance when it comes to work, life and family. In my eyes, it simply doesn't exist when you look at your life through the lens of the different chapters that make up your story. You will see an eclectic body of work: in some of those chapters, the demands of parenting dominate your every waking moment, while in other chapters you are consumed by work, business or your career. The term 'balance' denotes a neatly apportioned load, where each side perfectly complements the other. It implies that we have equal amounts of work and life, which is rarely true in reality. What I have learned is that having a family and having a career never quite align with each other over the multiple seasons of life. So how about we call it the blend instead? There will be times when there is a bit more work in that blend, and times when there is a bit more life within the mix. If you are working towards a career goal, then the blend may consist of more work in favour of your ambitions, and there is nothing wrong with that at all. There will be seasons where you absolutely have to lean in and go for it, like when you're starting a new role or going for a promotion. Conversely, there will be seasons where your family life takes priority, and that is more than okay.

The importance of breaking glass ceilings with a baby on the way and beyond

The facts speak for themselves. We still very much live in a man's world, and in a professional setting, it is still hard for women to progress in the same way as their male counterparts – and even harder for women who are mums or mums-to-be. These challenges can be further compounded by issues around race, socio-economic status, disability, sexuality, neurodiversity and age. Although we are seeing change, I am one of the many people who feel this change is not happening fast enough.

In the UK, there are only six female CEOs of FTSE 100 companies, and globally, women hold fewer than 24% of senior roles, according to research from Catalyst, a global non-profit supported by many CEOs and leading companies with the aim of building workplaces that work for women. Yet different sources of data show that women in leadership have a profoundly positive impact on businesses. Research has shown that companies with more women in senior positions are more profitable and more socially responsible, and provide safer, higher-quality experiences for their clients and customers.[1] In addition, there is a positive impact to the economy if household incomes reflect that both parents are being paid the fair market rate for their valuable skills.

Beyond the business reasons, it is the right thing to do to ensure that women, many of whom are mothers, have access to the same opportunities as men. As of 2019, three in four mothers with dependent children (75.1%) were in work in the UK, compared with 92.6% of fathers with dependent children.[2] So what is happening to all the mums in the workplace? Well, almost three in ten mothers (28.5%) with a child aged fourteen years and under said they had reduced their working hours for childcare reasons. This was only true for one in twenty fathers (4.8%). For some women, reducing their hours or stopping work is the right choice for them and their family, but for others it's a choice they'd rather not have to make, or would prefer to make on their own terms. It can hold women back from their true earning potential, and sometimes from pursuing dreams that are critically important to them.

One of the pieces of research that always spurs me on is from 2015. It shows that daughters whose mums worked are more likely to earn a higher wage, and sons whose mothers worked were more likely to spend time on family duties.[3] So, it is valuable for the next generation to have examples of mums rising through the ranks. And now seems as good a time as any to help accelerate the rate of change to create a fairer world for women, both now and in the future.

While this book is packed full of practical advice, I deeply appreciate that you won't be able to implement everything all at once, and you may not even be ready to implement any of it at all. And that is more than okay. As long as you start to understand that any narrative about working mums not being able to build successful careers is utter nonsense, and as long as you start to believe in yourself, then my job is done.

My story

I have been given this beautiful opportunity to write what I believe is a very important book for women. It's an incredibly exciting moment for me, because in many ways I have experienced so much of what this book talks about (both the good and the bad). I have been through (and I am still going through) the many ups and downs of working motherhood. In some areas, I have fumbled my way through it, making 'mistakes', learning lessons for the better; in other areas, I have achieved some of things I'd always dreamed that I would do, irrespective of having children. I am taking thousands of women on the journey with me and being inspired by the courageous individuals I meet. I still have a long way to go, but the journey of helping to empower women and mothers who dare to dream has been one of the best things that has ever happened to me, and I will never take this opportunity for granted. I hope that in these pages you find your voice, and the courage to always pursue what is important to you.

This book is so important to me because right at the start of my working motherhood journey, I faced some surprising challenges from different individuals: negative comments and assumptions about my ability to perform at work because my personal life was changing. Those experiences hurt, because I knew how committed I was to always doing my very best in anything that I did, but in many ways, they were also the wake-up call that changed everything. These experiences began to fuel my obsession with understanding just how women are able to grow in their career regardless of their motherhood status. This obsession grew into a desire to share as much information as possible to help women who wished to be mums understand the journey ahead, in a way that was engaging, relatable and easy to understand. I made a quiet but fierce commitment to myself to somehow turn everything I'd experienced into something positive. I'm so grateful for my amazing friends, lots of whom had babies at a similar time to me. Through many conversations about our working experiences while pregnant, they inspired me to start something, and eventually to give My Bump Pay a go. My Bump Pay is an online platform that I started to help women navigate their career journey, life goals and motherhood. I created it to help women achieve their goals with a baby on the way and beyond.

I don't think I have ever been as frank as that before. I've always left out my truth when telling the story of why I started My Bump Pay. But it would be remiss of me to write a book including the stories of so many inspirational people whom I admire and not share mine, because I know there are so many women who, at some point, have been doubted, treated differently or had the odds unfairly stacked against them because of a baby or the desire to have a baby. I'm all about arming women with the knowledge and confidence to go out there and kill it in their careers, while also taking on motherhood. If I can play a small part in helping ambitious women rise up the ranks and make the professional world a more equitable and fairer place to work for all, then this book has achieved its goal.

In the summer of 2018, I nervously sat down with a sheet of A3 paper and started drawing out what I wanted to create. At the time, it was just a website. The plan was that it would house tons of information to help women make vital choices about their careers. On the sheet of paper, I wrote words like childcare, reviews, family life, masterclass, giving back, maternity pay calculator, how do other women do it? I also sketched out a logo, which looked a lot like the logo I still have today. At this point, I had no idea how much of an impact this piece of paper would have on everything that was about to happen. It's funny, because I actually forgot about my late-night scribbles until two years later, when I found that piece of paper again while going through some old notes. Initially, I wanted to share the maternity policies of organisations and what it was really like to work for them as a parent. So, on my birthday, instead of painting the town red, I started sending out a survey to women I knew to help me do just that. I was eager to hear the views of women who were in my target audience, and begged them to forward the survey on.

I hustled my way through connections via Facebook groups in order to get a working website built that would soon become known as MyBumpPay.com. It was tough making it all happen on maternity leave, but somehow I did it, and launched it to the world in October 2018 through a newsletter and an Instagram post. Fast forward to 2022, and the community has grown to over 20,000 people. Hundreds of women have taken a My Bump Pay masterclass, which gives them the exact tools they need to smash the glass ceiling with a baby on the way and beyond. The results have blown me away: women finding the confidence to ask for the promotion they know they deserve before going on maternity leave; women receiving worthy pay rises and finding their voices, celebrating their achievements and advocating for themselves. Some of these women have the most incredible stories and have overcome some real-life challenges, like relationship breakdowns, personal grief or discrimination, and I find inspiration in their stories every single day. In this time, I have grown a lot. I started out as someone who was quietly ambitious, probably to my own detriment, and whose confidence was upside down. I've also found my purpose through helping others; it's helped me to evolve personally and professionally, and I now work at a large UK media agency and serve on the board. I'm not sharing this with you to brag. I've had many moments where I have struggled, battled imposter syndrome (something that still comes up), and almost given up on myself. But I want to encourage you, and show you that you can absolutely achieve the success that you dream of, too.

Chapter 1
Starting a family

The journey begins for so many of us with a number of questions. Questions like, do I want a family? Am I in the right relationship to start a family? When should I start a family? How will it impact my career? How long will it take me to fall pregnant? Will I be able to conceive naturally? What happens if I lose the baby or it takes me a long time to fall pregnant? Shall I adopt? How will work react? Will I lose my job if I have a baby? What if the person who covers my role takes my place and I have no role to come back to?

Women are faced with so many concerns when it comes to wanting a family as well as their career. Very often, we navigate these questions on our own and try to figure it all out with trepidation, little guidance and lots of confusion. Very few of us would bring up this topic of conversation with anyone at work, especially at this early stage. Yet all these questions lie at the crossroads between what we want for our professional lives and our personal lives. This chapter will start to unpack them, and help you decide when might be the right time for you to start a family, and what key things you will need to consider. We'll also look at conceiving and work, and baby loss and work.

I always knew that I wanted to start a family; in many ways, it was a non-negotiable for me. My husband wanted children too, and we shared the dream of having little ones of our own. Continuing to build my career was another non-negotiable in my life ambitions! I gave some thought to the timing, but I probably didn't think through it all as much as I would have done if I'd had all the information I have now at my fingertips. That doesn't necessarily mean I would have timed things any differently, but I certainly would have been way more informed as I headed into motherhood for the first time.

When should you start a family? What to consider when thinking about a baby and your career

I will start by saying that this is an incredibly personal decision, and also something that, timing-wise, we are never really in control of. No one but you can truly know when the right time is to start a family. I would encourage you not to just look at what others are doing around you when making your decision, as this is one of the biggest changes you will ever experience. I'm also incredibly aware that having a baby is rarely straightforward. The journey is full of ups and downs and emotional twists, all of which we will explore here. I'm hugely passionate about women going after what they want for themselves irrespective of having a baby, so whichever side of the baby coin you fall on, just know that building the life and the career you want is totally possible. You just have to be super intentional about building the life that you want for yourself, never take no for an answer, and believe in yourself even when things get tough. My hope is that the tips and the stories in this chapter can help you ask yourself some important questions that will allow you to arrive at the right decision for you.

So here is what the research says about starting a family and your career. I will warn you, it doesn't paint the rosiest of pictures, but it would be seriously wrong of me not to share all the facts. A study carried out by the US National Bureau of Economic Research looked at the Danish population and found that when a woman has children, it can create a 20% gender pay gap over the long term.[4] I know, you are probably reading that and thinking it's incredibly unfair! It is! Another Danish study, which looked at data from 2016, said that the best time for women to have their first child is between the ages of thirty-one and thirty-four if they want to limit the impact it can have on their earnings and, tangentially, their careers. The thinking is that, at this age, you are slightly ahead in terms of your career, whereas if you have a baby at a younger age, you may have to forgo opportunities that can propel your career.[5]

In many ways, this makes sense. If you're more established in your career when you add a family to your life, it means that you may be in a better place financially, you may feel more secure in your role and have a more solid career history behind you. All these things may be true. In other ways, though, having children earlier can also work out positively for one's career. Some women agree that, yes, raising children and working is incredibly hard, but having children slightly younger gives you the benefit of more time on the other side; as your children grow more independent, you have space to focus on leaning in to your career. There are always outliers to the debate, and I include myself in this because I had my first child outside of the thirty-one to thirty-four age bracket. There are advantages and disadvantages at whatever stage you decide to start a family, and I think it comes down to making a deeply personal choice that you feel happy with, using all the knowledge that you can gather, so that you arrive at the conclusion that is best for you. In this book, we will walk together through experiences, tips and tricks to help you have every possible chance of success whatever your age.

I don't believe in career ladders, because ladders imply a straightforward journey with equal steps. The reality is that our careers are full of wonderful and challenging twists, turns, pauses and side steps. So when thinking about your career and the timing of hopefully having a baby, I say: think about the big career milestones that you want to hit. For example, do you want to be a partner at a law firm, or become a non-executive director or head of a team? I would write down some of the attributes and skills you need in order to achieve those goals, in addition to a list of the people who can help you reach them. This will help you to understand some of what it may take to reach those milestones as you plan to start a family. It will also help you to identify points in your career that may be better suited for you in terms of starting a family. As you can see, I haven't given you a definitive answer, and that is because the reality is there isn't a perfect time to have a baby with respect to your career, because so much of it comes down to personal circumstances, including your chosen industry, your finances, your medical history and your route towards becoming a parent. There may be a natural point in your career journey where you feel more comfortable embarking on the baby journey, and that is a powerful and very personal choice.

My first child came at a time when I was responsible for a large team of forty people. The business I was in at the time had gone through a number of positive changes that I had spearheaded. I look back at my achievements before falling pregnant with my first child and I'm incredibly proud of everything I was able to accomplish at that time. I had led the business through a strong period of growth and had grown the team significantly.

However, I can honestly say a part of me was petrified that I might lose all the great momentum I had built up. Several questions constantly swirled around in my head. Would I lose my success capital? Would all my hard work be forgotten about? Was it the perfect time for my career? I didn't have any of the answers to those questions at the time. But I did know that having a family was deeply important to me, and I was determined to somehow make it all work to the best of my ability or at least to give it my very best shot. What I was confident of was that I still had a burning desire to achieve more, even though I was about to go on maternity leave. I learned so much during that time, which I will of course unpack throughout this book. One of the most important lessons that stuck with me about being pregnant and working is that you have to fiercely and proactively go after what you want to achieve. Don't leave it to chance.

The best way for you to still achieve your career milestones while growing your family is to be incredibly intentional about your career on your journey to motherhood and beyond. Lay as much of the groundwork as you can before starting a family, be mindful of what you can do while on maternity leave, and don't be afraid to be laser-focused on what you want to achieve and what is best for your family when you return. I will unpack how exactly to be intentional in this way, and we will explore the strategies you can put in place to enhance your chances of success.

I am team 'go for it' – grow your career and your family at the time that feels right for you. Blend it, make it happen, don't hold back! Don't put your dreams of having a family on hold for too long, because I strongly believe that work is the stuff that happens during life, so you very much have to pursue your life ambitions wholeheartedly where possible, and never have any regrets in your personal life because of your professional life.

Discuss it with your partner

If you are having a baby with another person, they are a huge part of your career/parenthood journey that shouldn't be overlooked. As you approach parenthood, it's important to establish the value of working as a team, especially if both of you plan on being working parents. It's so important because having a partner who is all in with you means that you can both support each other, and it also means that both individuals can continue with their careers and still play their part in raising children. In a team, different people contribute in different ways to help achieve a common goal, and it's no different when two people are bringing a new life into the world. Your partner is the most important person in your support network, and you shouldn't be afraid to openly discuss your ideas around being parents as well as your careers. If you are embarking on the parenthood journey alone, then you should be having this conversation with your support network. Before you start a family, discuss what is really important to you and your career ambitions, and how you can all work towards achieving your goals. How will you theoretically manage working towards big career moments with a family? Are there any non-negotiables – for example, do you want to work part-time? All of these points should be discussed well in advance. There is no way that you will see eye to eye on all these life-changing topics, but it's critical to go into it having an early idea of where the other person is at, even if they change their mind at a later stage.

Are you financially ready to have a baby?

This isn't about having thousands put aside in terms of savings. This is more about really understanding the financial impact of having a baby and really understanding your maternity pay policy. The moment you join a company, read their maternity policy inside out. I recommend everyone should do this, even if you are not sure about having children, for a few reasons. Firstly, there is a chance that you could be taken by surprise with a pregnancy, and so it is best to not be caught out. Secondly, you may be a line manager for someone (regardless of gender) who is having a child, so it would be super handy to know how the policies work. Thirdly, if you are planning for a little one, you need to know exactly how your policy works in relation to pay. I often recommend that women read it over several times and question anything they are unsure of. I have spoken to hundreds of women who haven't read their company's maternity policy in full, and then sadly realise that they don't qualify for maternity pay when it's too late – which can be an extremely stressful situation. Don't worry; I'll walk you through what happens if you don't qualify for maternity pay in Chapter 2. Fourthly, make sure your partner knows what they are entitled to as well in terms of leave. More and more companies have incredibly progressive parental pay policies for partners, and it would be a shame not to factor this into the equation when thinking about finances.

Lastly, you should read any company handbooks or additional policies around paid leave, as they may contain bits of information that are crucial to your decision-making. For example, policies around annual leave can impact how you structure your maternity leave.

Do you need to have lots of money saved to have a baby?

The short answer is no. You don't need to have tons saved to think about starting a family. I believe what is critical is being realistic about the big costs you could be facing along the way, especially when it comes to things like childcare, and also generally taking into consideration the fact that for a period of time, you will be on a reduced income.

Research from 2020 shows that it costs £152,747 for a couple to raise a child to the age of eighteen.[6] But I can promise you that you don't need to have all that money ready from day one. I think a good way to look at it is to think about it all in stages and not to get overwhelmed by the cost from the outset – otherwise you may never embark on having a family.

I can tell you now that when I had my little ones, we had some household savings. What did help me personally was knowing that during the pregnancy, I had some time to make a basic savings plan. I decided to put small amounts of money aside into another account, which I called my baby account, and this helped with some of the miscellaneous costs that can sometimes crop up during your maternity leave – for example, socialising with other parents. The second time around, I signed up to the app Plum, which helps automate your savings according to your savings goal, and this helped me massively.

You may have to make some changes to your lifestyle here and there, but having access to the right information will help you make prudent decisions when it comes to a family and finances. We will talk a lot more about money in Chapter 2.

Conceiving and work

The journey to getting pregnant is an incredibly private one, and so the phrase 'conceiving and work' can seem jarring because work is a more public territory. Very often, getting a better-paid maternity-pay package is linked to how long someone has been at a company, so naturally a lot of women have to think about conceiving in terms of how long they have been in a job.

I often get asked by women if they should move jobs while trying to conceive. I'm a huge believer that you should, where possible, make the choice to be in the organisation that is best for you, somewhere you are valued and where you can thrive. That sometimes means leaving a job and starting a new one, and on occasion the timings may not work out in your favour when it comes to maternity pay. It could be that you may not have been with a company long enough during your pregnancy to be eligible for maternity pay. That is a cost you personally have to weigh up. On the other hand, the impact of staying in a job that is detrimental to your wellbeing can have a profound negative impact on you in a number of ways, including the ability to conceive.

I think, where possible, it's critical to share the stories of women who have had positive experiences moving jobs while pregnant, and the steps it has taken to get them there. If not, how will we create and stimulate more progressive conversations and show organisations that, when handled well, the outcome can be largely a positive one?

Words of wisdom from Sagina Shabaya

Sagina Shabaya shared her words of wisdom and experience of securing a new role while she was seven months pregnant. Sagina is the head of inclusion, diversity and belonging for EMEA in London, at a global advertising and marketing agency. She is also the founder of 60 Min Career Coach, and has helped me navigate some important career moments.

I was seven months pregnant when I was headhunted for a fantastic role, right in the midst of the COVID-19 pandemic. Virtual interviewing turned out to be a real equaliser because just my head was in view. I didn't have the experience of walking into an interview room feeling judged, and I got the job based entirely on merit.

If you get a new role when you're pregnant, it's important to think about when you will disclose your pregnancy. Personally, I would never want to start working for an organisation or business without being honest or truthful, because that's one of my values. During my interview process, once I knew I really wanted the role and I understood what was on offer, I discussed my situation with my prospective employer before signing the contract. I was forthcoming and let them know that I would totally understand if it didn't work for the business, but I really wanted to work for them, and I got the job on merit. It was really nerve-racking, having to have that conversation, and in all honesty the cynic in me came out, and I just didn't think they were going to say yes. They came back with a response that just blew my mind. They said yes, of course, and were incredibly keen to discuss how we could make this work and what I needed to make it happen.

It is important to pick the right moment to share the news about your pregnancy, but hopefully once you have had the conversation, it's about planning ahead. You're in a powerful position to have a say in the plan – you can work to find someone to cover your maternity leave, for example. You could even use it as an opportunity to promote people internally. I was able to shape my maternity cover and have my role split between two people internally who were keen to get additional experience in other areas of the business. These two people were able to take six months from their roles to upskill in a new part of the business and cover my role. My whole experience made me want to shout about it a bit more, so I wrote a piece for my industry publication and got great responses. In many ways I am an anomaly, but it is important for other women and businesses to see that it is possible to make it work.

Having a baby is not the end. As women, we've got to start seeing and believing that. It's also important to have the confidence and self-belief. You have amassed the skills that you have amassed; your CV is incredible. You know the role that you're currently doing before you go off to have this baby, you've got that role on merit, and you have been delivering. It's about all the achievements that you've had to date. So, when you have this pause moment, see it as time to bond with your family and enjoy it – because that time goes really quickly, it's not that long, and you'll soon go back to work. There can be drastic changes in an organisation, but in many ways, you will still go back to many of the same issues – just a different day!

Infertility, baby loss and work

This is an incredibly sensitive topic, so if you find it triggering please do feel free to skip it. If you have reached this part of the book and you are thinking that this may not apply to you, I would encourage you to please read on, because you never know when you could be working with or managing someone going through baby loss.

One in seven couples may face difficulty conceiving,[7] and one in four women will experience baby loss.[8] It's staggering, it's heartbreaking, and yet it is the reality for so many. It really saddens me that it can be such an isolating time, and even more so when you are trying to manage your work life as well. So many women battling with this intensely difficult time find it complicated by the fact that they may not want work to know what they are going through for fear of being treated differently because they are trying to start a family.

I wish this was spoken about more openly in companies when thinking about employee health and wellbeing. The sad fact is that the majority of company policies are built around those who become pregnant successfully. As women, we know from our own experiences or those of friends and family that the journey can be complicated, and for many it can be a silent and painful one. Being the person to openly have that conversation at work can be incredibly challenging, and of course there is that deep-rooted fear that if people are aware you want to have a baby in the near future, then you will be treated differently and perhaps not have access to the same opportunities as those who aren't open about their desire to start a family. The data supports this. A survey from Fertility Network UK shows that 50% of women don't openly talk about their fertility treatment to their employer out of fear that the employer wouldn't take them seriously, and over

40% because of concerns about its negative impact on their career prospects.[9]

I'm going to share a few thoughts on how to help navigate baby loss and the fertility journey at work, as well as some words of wisdom from some incredible women who have been on this journey, and whom I admire greatly.

Tips to help with baby loss and work

1. Understand the current law

The current law differs based on the circumstances, so as hard as it is, it is important to understand the difference between a miscarriage and stillbirth.

Miscarriage: the spontaneous loss of pregnancy before twenty-four weeks of gestation.

Stillbirth: the loss of a baby after twenty-four weeks, before or during birth.

In the horrible circumstance of a miscarriage, under the current law, you won't be able to take maternity leave or be eligible for maternity pay. You can take sick leave, so if you need more than seven days off, it's a good idea to speak to your GP, and they can certify you the time that you need off for pregnancy-related illness.

If you were to tragically experience a stillbirth, you or your partner will be able to take maternity or paternity leave as long as you would normally qualify for leave. The same also applies to maternity or paternity pay.

Following a stillbirth, you would still have all the normal rights that someone on maternity leave would have.

I think the law doesn't quite cover the extent of how much the loss of a child can impact someone, directly or indirectly, in their career/working life. So it is great to see some companies go further than the law to support those impacted by loss. This is why I really encourage people to check what their own company policy says in this area.

2. Check what your policy says regarding baby loss

Channel 4 was one of the very first employers to implement a policy dedicated to pregnancy loss. This covered all types of loss, including miscarriage, stillbirth and abortion. In addition, it covers men and women who have been directly or indirectly affected. For example, they offer a minimum of two weeks' full pay for all kinds of loss. The broadcaster very much paved the way for other employers to follow suit. Slowly but surely, employers are starting to take note and are introducing such policies into their contracts.

It is certainly worth checking to see if your company has adopted a similar stance. Even if they haven't, I wouldn't be afraid to open up the conversation about introducing such a policy, especially if your organisation sees themselves as progressive, fair and supportive of diversity.

3. Consider a phased return

This may not be something your employer offers, but it is definitely worth having a discussion about it if you feel that you would benefit from easing yourself back into work. As an example, you could start off working three days a week, then gradually work your way back to five days a week.

4. Turn your camera off during virtual meetings

You may find it easier at first to be a part of virtual meetings with your camera off. This can help meetings seem less daunting, so they're a bit easier to take part in if you want to and feel up to it.

5. Be in control of how you want to share your experience with your colleagues

It is more than okay to choose if and how you would like to communicate your experience with your colleagues. You could decide to meet or speak to a few select colleagues before heading back to work if that would make you feel more comfortable. Equally, you could decide that you don't wish to talk about it. You can totally set your boundaries around communication however you see fit.

6. Practise self-care

Looking after yourself is one of the best things you can do. Dealing with loss can really take its toll, and so you do not need anyone's permission to look after yourself. Spend time doing the things that make you feel good, and do not feel any pressure to do things that you find difficult or upsetting. Don't be afraid to ask your loved ones to help you enforce boundaries. At work, you may want to consider having a conversation with your line manager to agree what boundaries you need in place as you ease back into work, and to ask for their help enforcing those boundaries.

7. Surround yourself with good people

If you have a parent and carer support group at work, they may just be a brilliant source of support for you.

Spending time with a trained therapist can also be beneficial. Lots of companies have an employee-assistance programme as part of their benefits, and you may find making use of the service incredibly helpful.

8. Partners

Even if you are not the one who has directly experienced the loss of a baby, it doesn't mean that you are not equally impacted. You will also be experiencing a grieving process of your own, and in many cases you'll be the first person to go back to work, which can be incredibly tough. My advice is to consider how you may want to implement any of the tips in this section to help you ease back into work. You will also need your own coping mechanisms and support network to help you adjust to this incredibly difficult time.

If you are a line manager or a friend of someone experiencing baby loss

Be kind, be supportive, be empathetic. Remember this individual did not choose to be in this position and so empathy will go an incredibly long way.

Acknowledging their loss can really help; it shows that you are aware of and sensitive to their situation. Asking how they are doing is extremely powerful, but don't push a full-blown conversation about what happened. Be open to the fact that they may not want to talk about it. Asking after their wellbeing is the kind thing to do.

What NOT to say

Some phrases can be really triggering, even though you may be searching for something kind to say. The following phrases are statements that people may find upsetting, so try not to make them.

'Everything happens for a reason.'

'You can always try for another one.'

'At least you weren't too far along.'

'At least you can get pregnant.'

Charities

There are some tremendous organisations doing incredible work in this space. Do look them up if you need further support.

- The Miscarriage Association
- Tommy's
- Sands
- Teddy's Wish
- Saying Goodbye

Fertility treatment and work

The number of women going through fertility treatment is on the rise, especially with more and more women delaying starting a family. One of the reasons for this is that we're spending more time building careers that require us to work long hours, or studying to improve our career outcomes. In addition, many of us are probably all too familiar with that children-versus-career conundrum, where we feel that we have to pursue a career to a certain level before introducing the idea of having children. Other reasons include not being ready, or not meeting the right person until a certain point in time. All of this means that women are having children later on in life, and when you combine this with the female biological clock, time is, frustratingly, not on our side. Most of us are incredibly aware that after thirty-five, our fertility declines. Plenty of women go on to have successful pregnancies beyond thirty-five, so it is not a total picture of doom and gloom. What it does mean is that as more and more women have children later, more women end up having fertility treatment to help them on their journey.

Fertility treatment is a huge undertaking that can really impact so many areas of your life, from finances to emotional wellbeing, relationships and work. So it's only right to address how to navigate fertility treatment and the workplace. There are so many different layers to this journey, but I hope this section helps you feel more informed if you need fertility treatment or have to support someone going through it.

Should you let work know about your fertility treatment?

You do not have to feel pressured to tell your employer that you are going through fertility treatment. It is a very personal decision. If you choose to, it might be a good idea to follow up any conversation you have in writing, documenting that you have let them know about upcoming fertility treatment and outlining any plans that you may have discussed with your employer.

How to manage fertility appointments and work

The law doesn't give you the right to time off for fertility treatment as it does for pregnancy-related appointments. Fertility treatment appointments should be treated in the same way as any other medical appointments.

When you know you have a few appointments coming up, I would make sure that expectations around what you need to deliver are incredibly clear between you and your manager. That way, you can focus on those deliverables, which will help you meet those expectations and manage good performance. If at any point you feel that you might struggle to meet those deliverables, flag any issues as early as you can. When flagging potential issues, I would have a few alternatives or solutions to suggest, if possible. For example, it may be that you can deliver, but you will need to work staggered hours for a period of time while you have your appointments.

This may also be a time when you will want to focus just on your main deliverables and step back from any other extra-curricular responsibilities, so that you can save your energy for the journey ahead of you.

Check to see whether your company has a policy around fertility treatment

Your company may have a policy in place around fertility treatments. More and more companies are offering this as part of their benefits package, which is amazing, and I hope even more companies adopt this approach in future. In the UK, companies like Clifford Chance, LinkedIn, Goldman Sachs, NatWest and Cooley have a policy of helping their employees with the cost of fertility treatments, to as much as £45,000. Your company's policy may also address this topic, and may outline additional support for anyone going through this process.

Support

It's more than okay to lean more on whatever support you have in place while you're on this journey. This could be your family, friends, colleagues, mentor or coach. Any kind of fertility journey can be extremely difficult, and you may need your support network more than ever before. I truly believe that no woman was made an island. In good times and in bad times, we need our support networks. Jaz Rabadia, a lady whom I know and deeply respect, talked to me about her experiences with loss, IVF and infertility, and the importance of having support around her.

Words of wisdom from Jaz Rabadia

Jaz Rabadia MBE is a senior executive within the STEM industry. In 2015, her brilliant hard work was recognised and she was awarded the status of Member of the Order of the British Empire for services to the energy industry and promoting diversity in STEM. Jaz shares her words of wisdom for anyone facing infertility struggles and navigating work.

While I am now a proud mother of a beautiful son conceived through IVF and a daughter conceived after multiple losses, I reflect on what I've learned on this journey of heartache, hope and self-discovery.

Regardless of how common infertility is, there is still a social stigma attached to the subject. In the South Asian community, this is amplified. It's for this reason I have been sharing my experiences to help shine a light on a subject that secretly affects so many of us. When experiencing infertility or loss, although you might feel that you are alone, my biggest learning from the entire process is that I was anything but alone. Actually, I've found that talking more openly about any challenge or struggle that you're facing, and sharing your story with others, is one of the most powerful things you can do. I found that in sharing the story of my challenging journey to motherhood, I have opened the door for other people like me to have the confidence to share theirs.

Struggling to conceive and coping with loss was very physically, mentally and emotionally draining. I couldn't face talking about it with people, mainly because I couldn't face them talking about me. But as I shared my story, I realised there was a whole community of infertility and IVF warriors that could relate to my experiences. They provided more comfort and strength to me than they will ever know.

When I wasn't up to talking, I would write things down. This became my therapy, helping me to celebrate the highs and cope with the lows. I think the best way for infertility to become less taboo is for more people to talk about their experiences so that we can learn from, understand and connect with one another. It is the most powerful tool available to us: we must normalise the subject, and that will help to make it easier for those who might undergo similar experiences in the future.

In my experience of managing IVF and work, I found that with IVF, timing is everything. The process has little appreciation for working mums, their schedules, or their prior commitments. This became quite a challenge to manage. I would always try to use my IVF calendar to plan work and meetings around my treatment.

Assisted conception is a very private process, but it can be hard to keep to yourself because of the physical and emotional toll it can take, as well as the practical considerations that need to be made, such as taking time off work to attend appointments. I remember psyching myself up for what I thought would be a difficult conversation with my manager. I thought that if I let slip that I was trying to build a family, I would be showing weakness, that perhaps they would think I wasn't as committed to my career as my counterparts, or that I didn't deserve that pay rise or promotion. Even though I knew my work environment wasn't like that, it didn't stop the doubts racing through my mind.

The conversation with my manager was fairly matter-of-fact. I explained to him that I had a series of upcoming hospital appointments, but I planned to make up the time I was absent from the office. I didn't ask for permission; I was frank about needing time off and offered a solution. My manager understood that something was happening that I wasn't comfortable talking about, but he was still supportive in giving me the time that I needed.

I think it helped that I am a senior manager in the business and that my time in the office was quite fluid. I can see how this could be quite challenging if you are more junior and perhaps in a fixed office-based role. But my advice to those in this situation is to be as honest as you can be.

My treatment required me to have days away from the business and time off at short notice. Thankfully, my employers were flexible and value employee wellbeing. Because of the conversation I had with my manager, I didn't feel guilty about taking this time, nor did it add to all the other stress my body and mind were going through. It made a world of difference. I also had a confidant at work, who helped me to endure the whole journey. Just being able to air my thoughts and emotions on a walk at lunchtime was a massive help.

When it comes to baby loss at work, I think a lot more is being done in this space, and there is a lot more conversation around how we make the workplace a safe space to talk about these types of topics. In the last six years, since my infertility challenges began, I have seen many more steps being taken to address supporting individuals in the workplace. It's great to now see initiatives such as miscarriage leave, formal fertility policies and infertility employee communities starting to emerge.

There were dark times in this journey, when I was doubting how I would get through the days and weeks, whether I had the energy or the fight within me. But prayer, faith and friendship helped me to build my emotional resilience and find the strength to make it through. My infertility has truly shaped the woman I am today; I am stronger, braver, and more thankful than I ever imagined possible.

Words of wisdom from Pippa Vosper

It's so important to talk honestly and openly about loss, as well as how one finds their way back to work after it, and I'm so grateful that Pippa shared her words of wisdom on this. After three years of trying to conceive naturally, Pippa and her husband decided to explore IVF. After a successful round, Pippa tragically lost her son Axel in 2017 when she was five months pregnant. She has written about baby loss online and in a series of pieces for British *Vogue*, and she is also the author of *Beyond Grief*, a much-needed book that covers every aspect of pregnancy and baby loss, from the practical to the emotional. It offers both an inclusive perspective and a guiding hand to anyone experiencing a loss of their own, as well as those who are trying to support them through it.

The workplace can be a challenging space following a pregnancy loss. If you experience an early loss, you may not have announced your pregnancy to colleagues, so your absence and distraction can be misunderstood or viewed negatively. You might not know your colleagues well enough to want to explain your very private news. If you had announced your pregnancy, a work environment can be a potential minefield of awkward or upsetting moments. Many people don't know the right thing to say and comments may come across as insensitive. Most companies are ill-prepared to support employees through pregnancy loss or fertility challenges; it is not an area that is greatly understood, and is often seen as an experience to be 'got over' in a short space of time. Currently, there is no statutory paid leave in the UK for pregnancy loss, so the options are to hope for a compassionate boss, take holiday dates or take unpaid leave. Employees in the UK are only entitled to paid bereavement leave following a stillbirth, which is classified as a loss after twenty-four weeks of pregnancy. In the past couple of years, several leading UK companies have announced their paid miscarriage leave policies, which reflects the need to acknowledge that these life events have a significant impact on women and men in the workplace. My hope is that more follow suit soon.

Self-employment is another, equally difficult, situation to be in when you experience pregnancy loss. I had just opened a new store, and returned to work only five days after I lost a five-month pregnancy, which looking back was insanity. I felt like I couldn't leave my lovely assistant at the time, because I knew the success of the business laid heavily on my shoulders. Sales figures were four times higher when I was there. In many cases, the personal expectation from those who have experienced pregnancy loss is that you just have to get on with it, which is very much how I felt. And it doesn't matter what stage you were in your pregnancy, it's all very traumatic. Five years on, going back to work so soon still feels like an inconceivable part of my journey, but at the time I felt I needed to do that. When you're self-employed, you need to work to make money, but your life has been deeply affected by this traumatic experience, and the last thing you want to do is put on a brave face and continue with your pre-loss work schedule.

Sadly, with early loss, many people seem to think it's not that traumatic or significant, and don't think of what could have gone before that – which, for example, could have been ten years of trying to conceive and eight previous losses of longed-for pregnancies. People in that position often get responses such as, 'At least it was early,' or 'You're so strong, I'm sure you'll feel better soon,' all of which are deeply unhelpful comments. So, *there are all these considerations to take into account as you try to find your way back to work. Considerations also need to be made for those who have colleagues living through loss or fertility challenges. It would be hugely beneficial if training for managers and HR departments included how to best support employees through pregnancy loss or fertility treatments.*

My final word of wisdom to anyone who may be going through baby loss, especially if it is at an early stage, is that it's your decision and choice around how much you share. Whether you say you are ill, or that you've had a bereavement, you don't have to explain yourself. You can talk about experiencing a bereavement without giving details. Take the hospital appointments that you need and the necessary time off. It can be hard to share such personal news with others, but I feel in many ways, honesty is the best policy. It's totally okay that not everyone would feel comfortable with that, but to be honest about the raw realities of it means others will hopefully understand just how much pregnancy loss can affect people, both physically and mentally.

Adoption and work

Adoption is so incredibly rewarding, but can be an intensely difficult and lengthy process. If you are exploring adoption, I would definitely read your company handbook or any policies your employer may have around adoption. Many companies provide guidance and support once the adoption is finalised, but what we don't see much of are policies to help people as they are going through the process. Like many of these decisions, this is deeply personal to you, and so you may not choose to discuss it openly at work until you are ready. People in this position to whom I have spoken have shared that they found that confiding in trusted people helped them immensely through the adoption period, with supportive colleagues offering a trusted ear, and supportive employers checking in on their wellbeing in relation to the adoption process and giving them the time off needed for various appointments.

When you take time off for adoption leave, you still have the same access to statutory maternity pay and leave that you would have if you were pregnant, as long as you are classed as an employee, provide evidence of your adoption, give the right amount of notice and are adopting through an adoption agency. The financial aspects of statutory leave are explained in Chapter 2. Only the prime adopter – so one parent – can take adoption leave, but you may be able to take shared parental leave during this time.

Starting a family is such a personal journey, with so many elements to consider, not just the ones that impact your career. I hope this chapter has helped to guide you on where you can begin in exploring the topic yourself or with your partner. I also hope that it has helped you to feel less alone if you didn't know where to start.

Chapter 2
All things money and babies

I initially started the My Bump Pay platform to help people understand all about money and starting a family, and what it was really like to work at an organisation as a parent. I wanted to lift the veil around maternity pay and be fully transparent about the money side of things – including what policies are on offer from different companies, and tips and tricks to help women arm themselves with all the information they need to put them in the best position they can be in before starting a family. This is a topic extremely close to my heart, mainly because I believe no woman should be financially disadvantaged because of having children. So I am excited to get into this topic and share as much as I possibly can.

In this chapter, we will explore: how much it really costs to have a baby; maternity pay and how it all works; tips to help you make the most of your money on maternity leave; shared parental pay; and the cost of childcare.

How much does it really cost to have a baby?

Once you get the amazing news that you are about to become a mum, I guarantee you that one of the first thoughts that comes to mind is money. The day after finding out I was pregnant, I remember sitting at my desk, reading my work maternity policy over and over and over again to fully understand how it all worked. At the time, the policy read that any employee who was pregnant would only be paid statutory maternity pay (I will explain exactly how that works shortly). Most of you will know that it isn't very much, so let's just say I became pretty good at Excel spreadsheets during that time, trying to work out how much money we would have, and how long I could afford to be off work for. It was at this time that I started speaking to many of my friends who were also expecting their first child, in order to find out what type of maternity pay they were expecting to get. I was shocked by the range, to be completely honest. At the very top end, some had access to ten months' full pay, and at the lower end it was around two to three months' full pay. It definitely sparked a desire in me to ask more and more questions around how it all worked at my company. Most importantly, I asked if there was a desire to review the maternity policy. While the company I was working for at the time looked into my request, I spread-sheeted away and worked out all manner of scenarios of how much it would cost us to have a baby on various hypothetical maternity pay options. So let's just say I went into this armed with a lot of information and possible financial scenarios.

I quickly discovered that there are many ways to approach having a baby financially. With baby number one, I was so tempted to get as much as I could that was brand new, because of course my firstborn deserved nothing but the best. I remember my dad brought me the John Lewis baby magazine to browse through after one of his many trips to John Lewis, and I was completely sucked in by all the shiny gadgets I could get that promised to make my life as a new mum much easier. I even went to one of those baby shopping days with one of my closest friends and our matching baby bumps, and bought a complete travel set with very little prior research and the quickest call to my husband to make sure he was largely on board.

One day, I got a call from my best friend, who said that she had some items I could use because her baby was about to outgrow them. Coming from my best friend, I thought, *Sure, why not?* She kindly gave me a Snuzpod, a brand of baby cot that can attach to your bed, which makes waking up in the night much easier for the duration of time that the baby sleeps in your room. She explained so wisely how items like this only get used for a short period of time, but so much money is spent on them that it's a shame to let them sit there and gather dust, especially when they're in perfect condition. Her words, although incredibly true, didn't really sink in until much later.

Six months into being a mum, I remembered that very conversation as I was packing away the beautiful Snuzpod she had so kindly lent to us. It was a light-bulb moment. It began to sink in that my son had quickly outgrown a number of items that we had splurged on. Furthermore, our experience as parents definitely wasn't enhanced because of all the brand-new gadgets we bought. We could have easily opted for nearly new items for lots of things, and could have done without other things altogether. What made our experience special was all the memories that we were creating as a newly formed family.

With baby number two, I took a completely different approach. I knew the things that I wanted to invest in and the things that I could borrow or spend less on. I can tell you that it was completely liberating having baby number two without feeling like I had to buy all this stuff.

Breaking down the numbers

From my many calculations, I estimate that it can cost anywhere from approximately £1,800–£4,600 to buy all the main things that you need (not including food) in the first year of the baby's life. This cost can be reduced further if you are particularly savvy with how you make certain purchases, which I will share some insight into. I have broken down all the main costs in a spreadsheet you can find on my website, the details of which are listed in the Resources section of this book (see page 325). I have ranked all the items that you will need in terms of priority. Priority 1 items are pretty much essentials. Priority 2 items are the things that are nice to have, or things you may want later down the line. Priority 3 items are all the lovely extras that you may want to indulge in (and there is no harm in doing so), but it's a good idea to have all the facts in front of you before you do.

The wonderful world of nearly new

With my second child, I loved exploring the world of 'nearly new': used items in brilliant condition that people typically sell online. I also love selling baby items that I no longer have any need for. Some of my favourite places to buy and sell are: Facebook Marketplace, eBay, Vinted and Vestiaire. You will be pleasantly surprised by the things you can buy and sell. For example, I have bought some lovely winter coats for the kids online, and I have sold a highly coveted Tibba and Marl baby bag. Selling is a wonderful way to make some money back that you can then save or put towards other items that you may need for your little one.

Maternity pay

Knowing how maternity pay works, along with understanding what maternity pay you may be entitled to, is critical. This part of the chapter references how maternity pay works in the UK. Every country is different, but some of the principles around how to manage your finances while on maternity pay will apply to everyone.

Lots of companies pay over and above what the government typically pays for maternity pay, which is called statutory maternity pay (SMP). Anything over what the government pays is called enhanced or contractual maternity pay. Companies will generally say what criteria you need to meet in order to be eligible for enhanced maternity pay. Typically, you have to have been working at a company for a certain length of time; for example, at least one year. All of this will be laid out in your maternity pay policy, and if you are not sure about anything, then do ask. If you don't want to ask your HR team, then maybe ask a trusted colleague. Watch out for any clause about potentially having to pay any money back if you do not return to your job after maternity leave. If a clause like this exists, it should be part of your maternity policy, but watch out, as it may be included elsewhere in your general employment contract or handbook in sections about paid leave.

Statutory maternity pay

Statutory maternity pay lasts for nine months. For the first six weeks, you will get 90% of your average weekly pay. For months three to nine, you will get either £156.66 (£172.48 as of April 2023) or 90% of your average weekly pay, whichever is the lower amount. If you are a visual person like me, the diagram below should help. The payments are typically paid in the same rhythm as your normal salary, and it starts from the first day of your maternity leave.

My Bump Pay*

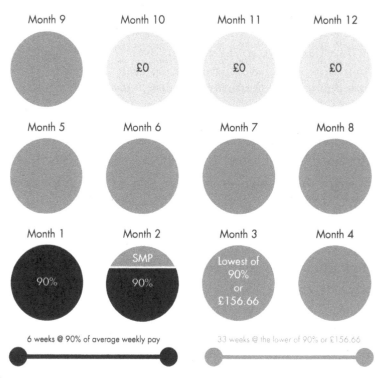

*Statutory weekly payments will be increasing to £172.48 as of April 2023

What are the criteria for statutory maternity pay?

There are a few key things you need to be aware of to make sure you receive SMP. To qualify, you need:

- to earn on average £120 a week
- to make sure you give enough notice – you must tell your company fifteen weeks before your due date
- to provide proof of pregnancy – you'll need a <u>MAT B1</u> form, which you can get from your doctor after twenty weeks
- to have worked for your employer without a break for at least twenty-six weeks

How do you claim statutory maternity pay?

You need to let your employer know what your due date is and when you would like to start maternity leave at least fifteen weeks before your baby's expected arrival. Your employer may want this in writing. In turn, the company must confirm your maternity leave start and end dates in writing within twenty-eight days. You need to provide your employer with proof of your pregnancy in order to receive SMP, although you do not need proof in order to take maternity leave. At least twenty-one days prior to your SMP start date, you should give your employer either a MAT B1 form from your doctor or midwife, or a letter from your doctor or midwife. Providing evidence is crucial, as without it you cannot receive SMP.

What to do if you do not qualify for SMP

Your employer must explain to you why you do not qualify for SMP within seven days of their decision via a SMP1 form. You may qualify for maternity allowance instead.

Maternity allowance

If you have fewer than twenty-six weeks of continuous employment, you will unfortunately not qualify for statutory maternity pay, but you may be able to get maternity allowance.

Maternity allowance is a government benefit for women who are currently working or have recently worked, but who are not eligible to receive statutory maternity pay. It is typically what those who are self-employed will receive. If you qualify for these payments, maternity allowance is paid directly into your bank account by Jobcentre Plus. You can't get it in addition to statutory maternity pay.

How much is maternity allowance?

You can receive:

- Between £27 to £156.66 a week for 39 weeks. Exactly how much you will be paid is based on how many Class 2 National Insurance contributions you have made in the 66 weeks before your expected due date.

To get the maximum payment (£156.66) you need to:

- have been registered with HMRC for at least 26 weeks in the 66 weeks before your baby is due
- and made Class 2 National Insurance contributions for at least 13 of the 66 weeks before your due date
- If you have made some contributions but haven't paid 13 weeks' worth, your maternity pay will be based on

how many weeks contributions you did make. If you haven't made any Class 2 National Insurance contributions, then you will receive the minimum of £27 a week.

To help you, there's a handy calculator on the government website that also details if you are eligible for maternity allowance. See https://www.gov.uk/maternity-allowance/what-youll-get

Enhanced maternity pay

The research I have done through My Bump Pay shows that, on average, those companies that pay enhanced maternity pay, pay sixteen weeks' full pay. So if we take that as an example, the sixteen weeks, full pay also includes statutory maternity pay. So each week, the government contributes the relevant statutory amount, and then your company tops up the remaining amount (well, technically, your company pays out the full amount and then claims back the statutory portion). The diagram below helps to explain it further.

In month one, you will receive your normal full pay, but you can see that what you will take home includes the statutory pay that you would be entitled to for that period, and then your employer will make up the rest to ensure that you get your full normal salary. As the months go by, you can see that the amount you receive in terms of statutory payments decreases a little, but your employer still makes up the difference in terms of your full salary for the period when you are

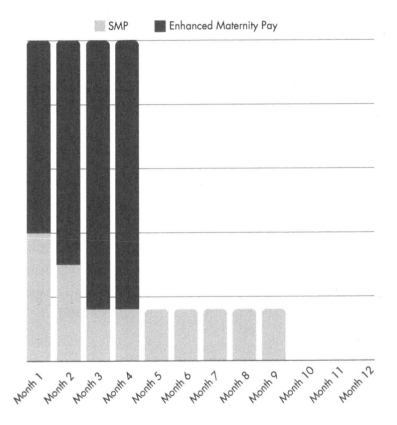

receiving enhanced maternity pay. Visualising it in this way should help clarify exactly how it works.

I do recommend asking for a schedule of payment so you can see exactly what you will get paid when. Misunderstandings around maternity pay can be frustrating and impact how you plan your time off. So, I am keen on women really understanding how it will work for them.

For example, if you get three months' full pay, then statutory payments, and the full-pay portion is inclusive of statutory payments, in effect you will get three months' full pay, and then for the remaining six months you will just receive your statutory payment. It's always good to clarify this, as it's easy to miscalculate.

If you have a policy that entitles you to ten weeks' full pay and sixteen weeks' half pay, you may be able to ask for the payments to be split equally over a period of time that is mutually agreed. For example, you may get your pay split into equal payments over six months. Every company is different in how they manage payments, but it is certainly worth thinking about what would suit you best and making an ask. Honestly, from experience, it is certainly worth asking.

Bonuses while on maternity leave

Research I carried out shows that approximately 55% of women receive their bonus while on maternity pay; 35% receive their bonus without any contractual obligations and 20% have some contractual obligation linked to their bonus. If your contract says that you are eligible for a bonus based on work that you have done, and that work is done before you go on maternity leave, then you should be paid that bonus.

I'm a big believer that everything is negotiable! If the language around what happens to your bonus while on maternity leave is a bit fluffy, I would certainly clarify what it means. And if the bonus isn't guaranteed, I still think it is worth asking your employer if it's possible for you to receive your bonus while on maternity leave, especially if your performance prior to your leave was in line with or exceeded any targets that you were set.

Create a maternity pay budget

There's no need to create one from scratch; I've done the hard work for you. You can find it in the downloadable templates on the My Bump Pay website, the details of which I have included in the Resources section of this book (see page 325). A maternity pay budget also lets you plan how long you can afford to take off on maternity leave.

By going through your normal budget and stripping back anything you don't need while on maternity leave, you will be able to see roughly how long you can afford to take maternity leave for. For example, the money I saved from not having to commute went towards my maternity pay fund. I found it super refreshing, and planning in advance took the stress away once the baby arrived.

Tips to help with money for your maternity leave

1. Automate your savings in the run-up to maternity leave

This is a personal favourite of mine. There has been lots of research around creating good savings habits that shows automating savings helps increase the amount you are able to put away. There are great round-up apps like Plum that can help you do this really easily. It automatically saves the spare change by rounding up money left over from your day-to-day spending. For example, if you spend £3.50 on a coffee, the app will automatically transfer 50p into your savings account, or even invest it for you. It's a great way to put extra money away before the baby arrives.

2. Use your annual leave towards your maternity leave

Depending on how much annual leave you have left before going on maternity leave, you can use it before your maternity leave kicks in. For example, you could stop working when you are thirty-eight weeks pregnant, and use two weeks of annual leave. This will mean that, for those two weeks, you get paid in full, and then your maternity pay will start on week forty. You could also do this towards the end of your maternity leave, using any unused annual leave to help boost your earnings. Have a chat with your employer to make sure they are in agreement with how you would like to use your annual leave. This method is incredibly common, and totally worth doing to help increase your income while on mat leave.

3. Use cashback sites for your baby purchases

There is a strong chance that you will buy a number of your baby-related purchases online. If so, then you should definitely make use of cashback websites where possible to help you save as much as you can on your buys.

4. Check if you're eligible for Sure Start

Sure Start is a maternity grant that pays £500 to help towards the cost of a new baby. You are eligible if this is your first child and if you receive any of the following benefits:

- Income Support
- Income-based Jobseeker's Allowance
- Income-related Employment and Support Allowance
- Pension Credit
- Child Tax Credit
- Working Tax Credit that includes a disability or severe disability element
- Universal Credit

---

5. Sell anything you don't need

You will be surprised what others pay good money for that you no longer need, so go for it and make the most of eBay, Vinted or Facebook Marketplace to earn some extra money for maternity leave.

Paternity leave and pay

It is worth briefly touching on paternity pay. It works in a similar way to maternity pay, and dads may be eligible if they are expecting a baby, adopting or having a baby through surrogacy. Dads can take either one or two weeks' paid leave; if two weeks are taken, then they must be consecutive.

Statutory paternity pay is set at either £156.66 (£172.48 from April 2023) a week or 90% of the father's average weekly earnings (whichever is lower).

Many companies offer enhanced paternity pay, which is more than the statutory amount, and some incredibly progressive companies offer the same amount of paid leave to men that they do to women.

Shared parental leave (SPL)

It does what it says on the tin: you can indeed share your maternity leave with your partner. It is designed to give you more flexibility about how your leave is split. I think it's great to have the option to go back to work at a time that suits you, and to leave your little one with your trusted other half rather than having to worry about childcare when your baby is at a young age. Not to mention I think it is brilliant that men have the option of experiencing extended paternity leave. I hope it makes more men empathetic to women who take time off work for caring responsibilities.

How does shared parental leave work?

Parents that qualify can be away from work together for up to six months, or they can stagger the leave and pay so that either parent is always at home during the baby's first year for a maximum of fifty weeks. The pay lasts up to thirty-seven weeks, and can be split too. The leave can also be taken in blocks. Parents are eligible to take a maximum of three separate blocks rather than taking all the leave in one chunk. You can choose to take these blocks at the same time as your partner, or the blocks can be staggered.

You need to be employed for more than twenty-six continuous weeks by the time it is fifteen weeks before the due date in order to take advantage of SPL and you must give your employers eight weeks' written notice of your intention to take it. Your partner needs to have been employed or self-employed for twenty-six weeks and must have earned at least £30 a week on average in thirteen of those weeks.

If you would like to take SPL, I would recommend letting your employer know as early as you can. SPL has low uptake, so lots of employers have only managed it a handful of times, or never at all. The more time you give them to work out the details, the better.

SPL is paid at £156.66 (£172.48 from April 2023) a week or 90% of your average weekly earnings, whichever is lower.

Childcare and finances

My husband fondly calls my children mortgage two and mortgage three, and he is right: having two children in nursery is no joke. Early-years childcare is eye-wateringly expensive, but also necessary for us to go back to work. Here in the UK, we have one of the most expensive early-years childcare systems in the world, according to research from the OECD.[10] The same research shows that the net cost of childcare is 30% of the average parent's salary. Lots of you may be nodding along as you read this, because you know only too well the crippling experience of paying childcare fees. I think that everyone needs to know exactly what childcare costs – not to put anyone off, but to ensure we are all fully aware. So, let's set it out: how much does childcare cost?

On average, sending a child who is under two to nursery full-time costs £1,050 a month, and part-time costs £551 a month.[11] This is the UK average; within the inner zones of London, the price can be almost double. We actually moved away from zone 3 after my youngest child turned one, and found childcare to be dramatically cheaper once we did! Once children reach three years old, the price of childcare tends to drop due to the change in staff-to-child ratios, and additional government support kicks in for most people, too, which brings some incredibly welcome financial relief.

In Chapter 6, I'll look in more detail at the pros and cons of different childcare options.

Childcare deposits

Lots of childcare arrangements will require some form of deposit, which can be equal to a month's worth of fees. So be aware that in the first month, you will have to pay a deposit and fees very close together, typically in advance of the child even starting. It's definitely worth asking when considering different childcare options if they need a deposit, how much it will be, and when it needs to be paid by.

> **What government help is on offer for childcare costs?**
>
> There are a few options for reducing childcare costs that are 100% worth making use of.
>
> ### 1. Tax-Free Childcare
>
> Under this scheme, eligible families will get 20% of their annual childcare costs (up to £2,000) paid for by the government.

Generally speaking, the tax-free childcare system tends to work out better for couples who have more than one child and therefore may have high childcare costs.

Eligibility for Tax-Free Childcare

You will need to have one or more children aged under twelve living with you. Adopted children are eligible, but foster children are not. You should work at least sixteen hours a week at National Minimum Wage (which works out to be £120 if you are over twenty-five). If you are in a couple, both of you need to be working sixteen hours a week. This does not apply if you're self-employed and you started your business less than twelve months ago.

To be eligible:

- You or your partner will need to earn under £100,000 per year. If you or your partner have an expected 'adjusted net income' over £100,000 in the current tax year, you will not be eligible. This includes any bonuses you expect to get.
- You must not be claiming tax credits.
- Make sure your childcare provider is signed up to the scheme before you pay them.

It's important to note that you have to confirm your eligibility every three months. If there are changes to your circumstances and your earnings change for some reason, for example maternity leave, it is worth checking to find out if you will still be eligible. Also, if you do earn over £100,000, it is a government requirement to file a self-assessment tax return, which you may find very helpful in terms of making sure that you have an accurate picture of your adjusted net income.

2. Universal Credit childcare help

If you're working (or both working, if in a couple) and you pay for childcare, you could claim back up to 85% of your childcare costs through Universal Credit if your family income is under £40,000. Before you even consider Tax-Free Childcare, it's worth checking to see if you're eligible for this help. However, if you get Universal Credit, you won't be able to get Tax-Free Childcare. The most you could get a month is £646 for one child, or £1,108 for two or more children.

3. Three years and older

When your child reaches three years old, you will be eligible for a further discount.

Usually, the price of your childcare provider will drop. In addition, children aged three and four are entitled to fifteen free hours of childcare each week. Those who qualify for Tax-Free Childcare will be eligible for thirty free hours of childcare. This only kicks in from the following term after your child turns three. For example, if the child is three in September, the discount starts the following January.

- Do check to see if your selected nursery offers government funding.
- You can find your nearest government-funded nursery using the government official search tool.

4. Child Benefit

Depending on your circumstances, you might also want to consider child benefits. You can get Child Benefit if your child is under sixteen, or under twenty and in approved education. For the oldest child, you can get £21.15, and for any siblings, you can get £14 per week.

There is a catch: if you or your partner earn over £50,000, you may be taxed on the benefit. Don't let that put you off, though; there is a plus side to Child Benefit when it comes to your pension.

If you don't earn enough to pay National Insurance contributions, (especially if you are looking after little ones) then Child Benefit will give you National Insurance credits, which go towards your state pension.

Don't forget the hidden costs

There are extra expenses that come along with adding a new life to the fold that are easy to miss. A fifth of expecting parents move to a bigger house to allow for their new addition! So you may be considering this. It's certainly not a must, because babies are quite contained for the first year or so of their life. So don't feel pressured to move straight away; you definitely have time. If you are thinking about applying for a mortgage, your mortgage provider may ask you about childcare costs. Some providers will look at childcare as a fixed cost, and may therefore deduct it from your salary when assessing how much they will lend to you for a mortgage. It sucks, but it is good to ask a broker about this during your mortgage process.

Other hidden costs may be things like life insurance, which I do certainly recommend but you may not have thought about until embarking on having a family. You may also be thinking about getting or upgrading to a new car, which is something else to take into account. Lastly, maternity leave can get quite boring and lonely. Socialising and baby activities and outings, such as coffees, lunches and yoga, add up. It's certainly worth adding socialising to your maternity leave budget.

Mind the pension gap

Pensions aren't headline-grabbing stuff, but stay with me. I think it's critical to understand how they work, and especially how the pensions of women who take time out of employment to have a baby are affected. I would love to shout from the rooftops about pensions so that no woman loses out.

Research from Prospect shows the gender pension gap was 37.9% in 2019–2020.[12] This is almost twice the amount of the gender pay gap. There are lots of contributing factors, such as women earning less than men and therefore paying less into their pensions. A huge contributing factor that goes under the radar is women earning less than the amount needed to pay National Insurance because they have taken leave from work for caring responsibilities. Those women might be losing out on National Insurance credits, if they aren't opting in for Child Benefit. What Child Benefit does is give you National Insurance credits which count towards your state pension. You need thirty-five years' worth of National Insurance credits to receive the full state pension, so it is really important to not have any large gaps that may affect this.

The reason why I think understanding this is so important is because women are still predominantly the ones that take time out of their careers to care for others. Yet, on average, we live longer than men. So there is a real need for us to have decent pensions and not fall into a pensions gap because of our gender.

The childcare investment

There is no doubt that for many of us, childcare is or will be one of our biggest costs, and it can significantly impact how we live and manage our finances. Initially, I found it hard to wrap my head around just how much it costs, but over the years I have reframed how I think about it, as much as it pains me to see the direct debit leave my account every month. I see it as an investment, as it allows me to go out to work, which I value massively. It allows me to provide for my little ones; it allows me to keep building on my career. Over time, my hope is that the money spent on childcare will be recouped because the years of continuous employment should mean that I will have been able to take advantage of promotion opportunities by not taking a career break. Paid childcare is not forever, and if you have free help from family and/or friends, cherish it! If circumstances mean that you aren't able to carry on with work, then don't stop investing in yourself; keep reading and learning, and keep your professional relationships alive.

The emotional impact of money and children

This is something that I didn't think about that much before having children. I had an intellectual appreciation that I would earn less, but I didn't really think about how I would feel not earning my normal salary. It's something I struggled with while on my first maternity leave. My husband and I truly are a team in every sense of the word, but I just couldn't shake the fact that I felt I wasn't contributing financially during this time. I think it's because I've always taken great pride in working hard and being rewarded financially, and for the first time ever, I was working really hard, at perhaps the hardest job I had ever done, but the compensation was different. It was certainly money-can't-buy rewarding; however, I didn't prepare myself for how I would feel emotionally about my earnings changing. My advice to anyone who resonates with my experience is just to remember that it is for a short period of time. If you choose to go back to work, you will start earning again. In this time with your little one, just know that providing the basics – warmth, shelter and food – is more than enough.

The future and schools

It is also worth thinking about the future in terms of schools, just so you know what options are ahead of you.

Do you want your child to go to nursery when they are old enough? Will you consider state or private schools? Where will you need to live in order to secure the school of your choice? How will another child affect this? How will you manage school hours and your career? Do your preferred schools offer after-school clubs, and if so, how much do they cost? I don't think there is any harm in thinking ahead and doing your research; for example, attending one or two school open days a few years ahead so you know what the options are in your area. Or, if perhaps there aren't any that you like, think about where you would move to based on future school options. You don't need to have any of the answers right now, but exploring different avenues ahead of time will help you make a plan to build a life that works with your family and career set-up.

> **Words of wisdom from Davina Tomlinson**
>
> I love that I've had the opportunity to share this advice with you about finances and raising a family. Ultimately, I'm incredibly passionate about women not missing out financially because they don't have the right information. But it's not all about our children when it comes to the pennies and the pounds. I love the advice Davina Tomlinson, founder of rainchq and author of *Cash is Queen*, which helps women build financial resilience and sustainable wealth, shared with me so eloquently below.
>
> *To use an airplane analogy, if I could give you one piece of advice about money and motherhood, it would be to make sure you put on your own oxygen mask first. By that, I mean don't neglect your personal finances in the spirit of maternal martyrdom.*
>
> *Of course, there are obvious financial planning tips to make sure your babies get off to a flying start, from Junior ISAs to (believe it or not!) child pensions, but if your own finances are on the precarious side, it will be impossible to establish any of these things for your children and maintain them over the long term. All this will do is add to the already long list of worries that all mothers invariably carry when it comes to their kids.*

And while this may seem like a no-brainer, you'll be surprised how many of us think the right thing to do would be to prioritise our children's finances first, in an act of selflessness that ends up putting us at the bottom of our own to-do lists. The result? Your child's junior ISA is away and flourishing with you struggling to fund it; meanwhile, you've barely got enough money in your pension to fuel a basic retirement. Not only will this store up problems in future given the retirement gap that already exists between men and women, but potentially, the very people you're desperately trying to protect could end up having to carry the weight of responsibility for your financial wellbeing as well as their own, a situation that none of us wants.

This doesn't mean you should forgo financial planning for your kids, not by a long stretch. Planning with your partner for dependants is a crucial part of the parenting journey. But don't embark on this journey alone, and don't let it overwhelm you. Be clear on what capacity you have to save and invest on their behalf, and don't commit to anything you cannot afford to sustain over time.

Remember: your financial security is their financial security, so it makes sense that you stabilise yours first. This may mean making sure you have good life insurance or critical illness cover in place, either privately or through work, so that your family will always be well taken care of financially in the event of unforeseen circumstances. It means making a will so that everyone is clear on your wishes and how you would like your *children to be looked after if you are sadly no longer here to look after them yourself. Matters of mortality and morbidity are upsetting to contemplate, I know, but if there was ever a time to really get to grips with these issues, it is now.*

Just as we must not neglect the rest of our self-care when we become mums, it's vital that we recognise our financial wellbeing is part of this too. After all, motherhood is challenging enough – let's not add money worries to the mix!

Words of wisdom from Clare Seal

Clare Seal is very well known on social media as @myfrugalyear for sharing the journey of her debt, which struck a chord with thousands of people online. She writes about the challenges of millennials and parents around money and debt. She is also the author of *Real Life Money*, *The Real Life Money Journal* and *Five Steps to Financial Wellbeing*. Her words of wisdom are spot-on for anyone trying to navigate family and their finances.

There are a couple of things I think are quite important. The first thing being, properly read into your rights and what you're entitled to. Make sure you know what your maternity package is, and talk to your partner about shared parental leave and whether that's something that you might be able to do – especially if they work for a company that offers better parental leave than yours does, because that can be a really nice way to smooth things out financially.

It's important to plan financially when it comes to expanding your family. It's also important to be aware that there are so many things that can happen when you have a child; so I think it's great to have a plan, but maybe don't be too wedded to it in terms of finances, because you may be trying to start a family and then end up with twins or multiples, and then obviously the costs really change. Or, you may not be well enough to continue working; some people have hyperemesis or a condition that means that you can't work for as long as you would intend to. So try to remember that sometimes pregnancies or the adoptive process can just throw curveballs in that sense. The main thing I would say is try to save as much as you can, not even necessarily because the stuff you need for a baby is super expensive (you can buy a lot of things second hand) but more so that you can have a bit of a financial buffer, which for many is incredibly valuable.

I'd really advise not following too many 'mum and baby' Instagram accounts, because it can make you feel that you don't have all the gear that you need. A tiny baby needs very little; it's more helpful to have a bit of a financial back-up if you can. Also, it's worth mentioning that a lot of people really struggle with the fact that maybe this might be the first time they're relying on their partner for money. If you've got some kind of back-up savings, they can really help to ease that anxiety.

If you're planning on taking a bit of a career break before returning to work, or your partner is, please, please talk to your partner about pensions so that you avoid missing out on earnings for your pension. Have a look at how much you can put aside and make sure that the burden of that is spread fairly across the two of you. This is a great conversation to have in advance, if you're in the kind of fortunate position of planning your family before it is sprung upon you – which did not happen to me.

Finally, you might want to think about saving for your children for when they're older. If you are planning on putting money aside, there are loads and loads of different options, but you could look into a Junior ISA, into which you can pay up to £9,000 a year tax-free. Because you will be saving over a very long period of time, it helps to mitigate the risk of investing, and it could end up being something really meaty that you can give to kids to help them start out when they're a little bit older.

Those would be my words of advice for anyone trying to plan for a family and thinking about their finances. As a caveat, I don't know very many people who haven't found it a stretch financially to have children. Please don't think you're doing anything wrong if it feels like a stretch, because it is for most people. And I would just really urge you not to get sucked into that comparison thing, like, 'So-and-so's kids go to Water Babies', or 'They're going to Rugby Tots', or 'They have the Stokke cot', and all of that stuff. Children don't really care about material things, and babies certainly don't care about posh *swimming lessons. So try to bear that in mind, because the stress of having spent beyond your means can add more pressure to what is already quite a life-changing period. It can be really, really hard. So I would say if you find it a stretch, that's really normal. Just try not to compare yourself to other people, because you don't know what their circumstances are.*

Chapter 3

Building a successful career during your pregnancy

Pregnancy is a time of such profound change, but also one that I think is a great opportunity to lay the foundations for the next phase of your professional journey. In this chapter, I will explore how to best communicate your pregnancy at work, and share a trimester-by-trimester guide to help you move towards your career ambitions during this time. We'll also explore a maternity leave checklist and the foundations for a strong return to work. A side note: while lots of this chapter applies to pregnancy, there are of course other ways of becoming a parent, but the key principles still apply.

I've always been a firm believer that women can achieve their career dreams when pregnant, in part because my mother worked so hard while raising us. I was born in the bustling and vibrant city of Lagos, Nigeria, and moved to the UK with my parents at seven months old. I am incredibly proud of my Nigerian heritage, and growing up in the UK with a variety of influences has had a deep impact on me, my drive and who I am as a woman and a mother. One of the biggest influences on the way I see life has, of course, been my parents. They are incredible people. I am biased, yes, but if you were lucky enough to know them, I know you would agree. From as young an age as I can remember, I have watched them graft to build an incredible life for our family. I hugely admire that they migrated to a new country and retrained to be pharmacists, all with two young children.

There is a special photo I have kept on my phone: it's a picture of my mum and a few of her friends in Sunderland. My mum is carrying my sister, who was just six weeks old, and one of my mum's friends is carrying me. I would have been under two at the time. Back in the early nineties, Sunderland was where pharmacists would take their qualifying exams. My parents were pharmacists in Nigeria, but chose to explore new opportunities and qualify in the UK also. Their final exams took place six weeks after having a new baby. Since then, they have both gone on to build successful careers and businesses. I often look at that photo to remind me of the huge sacrifices my parents have made to give their family the very best. It also spurs me on! Because of the brilliant example they have set for me, I feel like I have no choice but to push myself to do the best that I can for the benefit of those around me. In African culture, the notion of family is extensive; it includes second, third or fourth cousins, friends and even distant relations. Because of all this, I have always felt that I would never let having children hold me back from achieving my goals; I believe that my goals aren't there to serve me, but to provide for my family and impact those around me. In many ways, this helps to explain this book and why I am so passionate that anyone who is pregnant or expecting a baby can go ahead and achieve their dreams and ambitions. Yes, you have to be strategic; yes, you have to work hard; but it is totally possible to have career success while you are pregnant and beyond.

How best to tell work you are pregnant

Spring 2017. I can't remember the exact date, but I do remember going over and over in my head how I would tell my boss that I was pregnant. I knew he would personally be happy for me, but my goodness, did I deliberate on all the different ways I could say 'I'm pregnant' while still keeping it professional! The weeks before that were quite difficult; I felt like I could just about get by during my first trimester. I didn't have any pregnancy-related sickness, but I did have extreme fatigue. Many days, I felt like I had no energy, or like my head was spinning as if I were on a rollercoaster while I was on the Tube. The commute in those early weeks of pregnancy (pre-twelve weeks) was not fun. I used to wear a 'Baby on board' badge on the Tube, but as soon as I got to Charing Cross Station, I would take off my badge, hoping no one would notice. I needed a seat so badly, but I was petrified of bumping into someone from work. I didn't want anyone to know my news until I was ready.

At the same time, I also felt that I was in a catch-22 situation. Some days, I just didn't feel like myself, but I wasn't ready to say anything. I also felt a lot of pressure not to say anything before twelve weeks, because I thought you 'had' to keep it secret until then.

Fast-forward to 2019. Pregnancy-related sickness struck me with my second pregnancy. I'm not using the term 'morning sickness', because it is rubbish and outdated. I learned the hard way that being sick during pregnancy can hit you at any time of the day. It was not a fun time for me at all. I would arrive at the office feeling queasy and possibly having thrown up on my way into work; even the smell of after-shave would make me feel nauseous and leave me wanting to gag. Quite honestly, I really struggled getting through the day in those early weeks, keeping up with the standard of work I knew I wanted to deliver and trying to conceal the changes happening to my body. Six weeks in, I cracked! I was done with suffering in silence. Pretending I was okay was only causing me more added anguish and stress. So I spoke to my HR manager, and shortly after spoke to my boss. I was so glad I had that conversation, as it then meant I could speak openly about making adjustments to my working day so I could still deliver in my role and be there for my team. It was right for me at that time.

I know this can feel like such an overwhelming moment, so I want to share some handy tips to help you tell your news with confidence.

The dos and don'ts

Don't let your boss or line manager hear the news through the office grapevine. News always spreads fast at work, and you'll be outed without having had a chance to share it in your chosen way.

Don't rush it, unless you really have to. Even though there is a well-known school of thought that says you should wait for your twelve-week scan before telling anyone, sometimes it's really hard to hide and not discuss your situation if you are dealing with crippling pregnancy-related sickness. If you do choose to share your news before your first trimester scan, then I would be really specific about whether you would like the news to be communicated to others. You may want to explicitly state that your news should not be discussed any further. Before twelve weeks in pregnancy is a really sensitive time in terms of the viability of a pregnancy, and so the news should be managed sensitively.

If you feel good and you are not 'obviously' pregnant, then choose a time in your pregnancy when you feel most comfortable discussing it. Remember, you may be outed if you sit on the news for a really long time, as you can only blame it on 'a bug' for so long.

Do think about when would be a good time. You may feel more comfortable sharing the news after a big work milestone has been hit; for example, once a big deal has been closed or after your performance review.

Do book a meeting; don't mention it in passing. It's super-important news and shouldn't be treated as an 'oh, by the way' bit of information. Schedule a chat to tell your boss, and if the chat is in person, then go somewhere private and quiet, where you won't be disturbed or distracted.

Do prepare for your chat. Think about whether you have any questions that you would like to ask. It's so easy to forget what they are in conversations like this, so it is totally okay to write them down. Put yourself in the shoes of the organisation or your boss, and think honestly about all the questions they may have. They may not ask them during your chat, but they will be thinking about them. So it's always smart to go into these types of conversations ready, just in case these questions do crop up. Consider how your pregnancy and impending maternity leave may affect the business and their objectives, and be ready to share some early ideas or options around how you want to manage your pregnancy and your role. For example, if you have ideas about how your maternity cover should be handled, then do share them. Be proactive, be the solution; it goes a long way. I think in these situations, it's better to have as much input regarding the road ahead as possible, rather than just dealing with whatever set of cards you're given. Being the captain of your fate is extremely powerful in managing your career, especially when pregnant.

Do have some facts at your fingertips when asked, such as your due date and your initial thoughts about maternity leave. You may be asked in that meeting how long you are thinking about taking off for maternity leave, or when you would like your leave to start. You don't have to give an answer then and there, but I also don't think you should withhold information just for the sake of it. Be cooperative and mindful that they are probably trying to get an early sense of logistics for business planning. As an example, you could say at this stage, 'It is still very much up in the air, but I think that I might want to take between ten and twelve months.'

Do follow up your conversation in writing. An informal email to thank the person for listening and answering your questions around your pregnancy will do. I think it's good practice to document these milestone conversations.

Don't apologise. You have done nothing wrong. An apology will diminish the impact of what you have to say – plus, it's wonderful news!

What should you actually say?

This is possibly one of the most nerve-racking conversations that you may have in your career, but everything in this chapter should really make it much easier. Here are a few examples that you could take and adapt to your conversation style to help you. You don't have to use any of these, but they are helpful if you have no clue where to start.

'I wanted to share some exciting news: I am expecting a baby in [month]. I have been thinking a lot about how this will impact the team, so I have pulled together a plan about how my absence can be managed smoothly to ensure that we are meeting our targets.'

'I'm excited to let you know that I am pregnant and expecting a baby in [month]. This won't affect [insert current projects that you know you are able to deliver on]. I have given a lot of thought to my leave, and I think I would like to take between x and x months off. I am dedicated to a seamless transition before I go off on maternity leave, and I'm looking forward to returning after my maternity leave.'

When do you have to share the news?

You need to let your employer know that you are pregnant fifteen weeks before your baby is expected to arrive, so that is when you are around twenty-five weeks pregnant. If you miss this deadline, then you won't meet part of the criteria for maternity pay.

What if the news doesn't go down well?

The vast majority of employers will be pleased to hear your news, but occasionally you may not get the reaction you'd hoped for.

Remain calm and professional, and try not to worry; it is illegal for a company to sack you or treat you differently just because you're pregnant or plan to go on maternity leave. However, if you really are concerned, I would keep a record of any negative conversations or interactions that have happened since sharing the news of the pregnancy. If you need further advice, then there are some brilliant resources that you can turn to:

Pregnant Then Screwed: https://pregnantthenscrewed.com/

ACAS: https://www.acas.org.uk/

If you are concerned that the news of your pregnancy may not go down well, then it might be worth waiting to share your news. This then proves you're still able to effectively do your job, irrespective of being pregnant.

Nailing your career during your pregnancy, trimester by trimester

First trimester

Your first trimester of pregnancy will, in many ways, often be the hardest. You may be experiencing some difficult symptoms, and you probably haven't told many people. Make sure you listen to your body; the most important thing is your new baby and taking care of yourself, including being realistic about what you can manage at work. If you are not experiencing any major symptoms, then you can continue on pretty much as normal. If things are challenging, then do think about what adjustments you may need to make to help you still perform in your role. This could be working from home, adjusted working hours to help you with the commute, or maybe even slightly different tasks if you have quite a physically demanding role. In addition to this, focus on the tasks that really add value to the business. For example, if you have taken on extracurricular tasks, like heading up a committee, and you are experiencing a difficult pregnancy, then consider stepping back from additional responsibilities that are not core to your role and that take time away from you performing important functions. Save your energy for the tasks that really matter and add value.

Get crystal clear on the expectations of your role

Now is the time to get crystal clear on what the expectations around your role are. Do you have clarity around what excellence looks like? How are you performing against those metrics? How do key people in your organisation think you are performing against those metrics? If you don't have clear answers for any of these questions, I would strongly encourage taking steps towards gaining clarity in your first trimester, as this will really set you up for success.

I really encourage documenting all of this. Break down your role into different tasks that you regularly have to carry out, and against each task, write down what excellence looks like. Then write down and keep a record of your achievements for each task as you progress in your pregnancy. This document will become like your performance bible during your pregnancy, and you can use it throughout your career. If you were already in discussion about your progression at work before you became pregnant, then I would say this exercise is critical. It will enable you to show your performance against any criteria set, and will help you evidence your achievements with ease.

Use your first trimester to get really clear on your goals and what you want to achieve during this time. Work at a pace that suits you; this may not be the time to push, but if you feel that it is important to you to keep working towards your goals, then absolutely go for it.

Handling pregnancy sickness when you haven't shared the news

More and more of us are working remotely and so this may be a good time to make good use of your working-from-home days. If you have any flexibility around how often you work from home, you may find this helpful in terms of managing your symptoms under the radar.

Avoid anything that sets you off. For me, it was any musk-type fragrances and motion – and there were some random triggers too. As soon as I could identify these, I avoided them and it helped me massively.

Adapt your commute. If possible, try changing your commute times to help you avoid rush hour or travelling when you know you feel most unwell. If you don't feel comfortable getting a 'Baby on board' badge, then order a 'Please offer me a seat' badge from TFL for the commute. You might also want to keep some paper bags, tissues and wipes handy, just in case you are sick on the way in. If your sickness is crippling, do see a doctor to see if there is anything further they can do by way of support.

Second trimester

Start crafting your plan

After your twelve-week scan is a good time to start crafting your plan regarding what you want the remainder of your time at work to look like. You've probably been thinking about it already, but writing it down will really help you to refine it and make it actionable. Map out key milestones and think about key stakeholders who you might need to tell. Do you have an idea about your maternity cover? If so, flesh that out and come up with an actionable plan.

You don't have to have all the details just yet, but start to think about ideas and solutions to what can make your maternity handover as smooth as possible. Reading through this book can certainly help you form a plan so you can excel during this time.

Start thinking about childcare

Please, please, please don't leave childcare to the last minute. Chapter 6 is full of helpful information to guide you through your childcare search. Waiting lists for some childcare providers are years long. We put our name down for our son when I was sixteen weeks pregnant, and we were still told that there wasn't a space at our preferred nursery. It worked out in the end, but it was stressful! Book a few tours in your second trimester and review all the options available to you to help you make your decision.

Start thinking about your village

You can't make this journey alone. Having the right support network around you is invaluable. I think mum friends are like gold, and can lead to lifelong friendships. I feel so incredibly lucky to have my group of friends. There were twenty-one of us in total having babies in 2017, and they have become more like my sisters. They remain an amazing support to me even now as our babies have grown up into little people. Have a think about whether you would like to do a prenatal course, such as NCT or Bump and Baby, as it can be a great way to meet other mums. You might want to look into other options, such as apps like Peanut (see page 303), or you could join a parenting group at work. Whatever works best for you; just find people who you can make this journey with.

Get all your documents in order

This is the time when you need to get your MAT B1 form from your doctor or midwife to medically confirm your pregnancy. You need this document as part of the criteria to get your statutory maternity pay (see Chapter 2). Once you submit it to your workplace, it's a good idea to follow up in writing to confirm that they have received your form. Shortly after, it is good to confirm the details of your pay and ask for a maternity pay schedule so you have full clarity of what you are getting paid when.

Third trimester

Prep for maternity leave

You will have certain stakeholders that you need to think about when preparing for your maternity leave. They could be your team, your manager, your clients or wider influential stakeholders that you work with. You may need a slightly different approach to managing a smooth handover depending on whom you are sharing the details with. So leave plenty of time to get this done. I would start at the beginning of your third trimester.

Give work a heads-up on when you plan to return

You don't have to legally let them know until eight weeks before you plan on coming back, but it's helpful to give an estimated date so your organisation can plan for your return. Close to the time, you can agree a confirmed return date.

Look after yourself

This applies to all the trimesters really, but especially the third, because at this point the baby is growing fast, and you might be feeling more tired. If you've got bags of energy, go for it! Just remember to listen to your body and your baby. Your hospital appointments also become more frequent towards the end. Whatever you do, do not miss antenatal appointments for the sake of work. By all means, reschedule them, but do not completely miss them. Nothing is more important than your health and the health of your baby.

Create your handover

Any good handover is jam-packed with information. If you think there is too much detail, then, good, you are on the right track. The more detailed, the better, as you don't want people contacting you while you're on leave to ask you lots of questions. I recommend chatting through your handover document with any key people, and then sending it via email afterwards so that there is the opportunity for questions and clarification. Handle your handover in a way that you would like others to hand over to you if you had to take on a new role or responsibilities. Include in your Maternity Leave Checklist (see page 91) information on how you would like to be contacted in emergencies and define what constitutes an emergency.

Discuss your return

I feel it's really important not to shy away from talking about your return to work. Yes, your circumstances may change massively after having a baby, and you may not return, or you may not return to the same team or business, but I think if your career is important to you, you need to address it head-on. Don't ignore topics like this and allow people to make assumptions about what you want your return to look like, because the likelihood is that their assumptions will be very different to what you want and what will allow you to thrive. You certainly won't have the details of your return clear just yet, but it's a good time to discuss options, particular projects you want to be a part of, or any goals you may be working towards.

Take advantage of your KIT Days

I'm a huge fan of keeping in touch (KIT) days. You can work up to ten days during your leave, and their primary use is to keep in touch with what is happening in the business to make it easier to transition back. I think they are brilliant for so many reasons. First of all, they are paid; even if you work for just a portion of the day, you will still get paid for a full day! Secondly, they help you to stay in the loop with what is happening at work, which really does help to boost your confidence. Thirdly, they are great for visibility, and you can even use them to do training or attend important meetings. KIT days are an excellent way of reminding people in the organisation of your value. My advice is to keep in touch even if you are undecided about whether you would like to go back or not. Let your boss and HR know that you want to take advantage of your KIT days, and then you can discuss some ideas around how you would like to make use of them.

KIT day ideas

- attend staff or team meetings
- attend client meetings
- attend training days (useful if you have mandatory training requirements)
- settle back into work (including the commute)
- try out new childcare arrangements
- provide emergency cover for your team

Run through your Maternity Leave Checklist

Finally, at around thirty weeks, I would start going through your Maternity Leave Checklist to make sure you have everything in order, especially so you're covered if the baby comes early. Here is a handy list of things to run through before you go on maternity leave:

Maternity Leave Checklist

Handover. Has your handover been agreed, and has everyone who is covering been briefed on their responsibilities?

Give everyone an opportunity to ask any last questions, and discuss if and how you can be reached for any emergencies.

Conversations with stakeholders. Have you spoken to all key stakeholders to make them aware of your leave? Ensure that they too are comfortable with the handover plan and give them a chance to ask questions.

Keeping in touch (KIT) days. These are totally optional and an agreement should be reached between yourself and the business about how they should be used. It's a good idea to discuss your KIT days in advance. They are a great way to stay in the loop. Many people find them easier to do towards the end of their leave, when the baby is a bit older. The time should be paid at your normal salary rate.

Additional benefits. Check to see if there are any additional benefits that apply to new mums that you may not be aware of. If you have health insurance, you may want to ask ahead of time how to add your new baby to your policy (if possible).

Parent networks. Check if your organisation has any parent groups that you can be a part of for additional support, or whether they have a baby buddy scheme. If not, you can certainly look into setting one up; it could be as simple as a WhatsApp group.

Email. It's a good idea to create smart email rules, where emails are automatically filed into different folders so that your inbox isn't too overwhelming on your return. Put on an out-of-office response, and record an appropriate voicemail greeting on all phones that you may have linked to the business.

Performance reviews. Find out when any performance reviews are taking place if they are happening while you are on leave, and ensure you are included in any processes. Also check what your organisation's policy is around bonuses during this time.

Annual leave. Check how your organisation handles any unused holiday days. Many women choose to use their annual leave at the start and end of their maternity leave. It's good to have a chat about your options ahead of time.

Flexible working. Check what your company's policy is on this ahead of time, and speak to others to find out what arrangements have worked well for them and the business in the past.

Maternity pay. Check when and how you will be getting paid. It's helpful to ask for a schedule of pay that details exactly what you will be paid in each month.

Set up your out-of-office. A simple step, but easy to forget. Be sure to include who is on hand to cover any queries. It is fine to list different people for different matters.

Smashing your career goals while you are pregnant

I wholeheartedly believe that it is 100% possible to perform at work while pregnant if you are experiencing an uncomplicated pregnancy – you may just have to tweak how you approach things, and you've got to be intentional. I'm not going to pretend any of this is easy; it takes a lot of hard work and focus. I think society expects us to slow down once we find out we are pregnant – or, even worse, it can write us off. But I have seen, time and time again, women work hard to define their own success with a baby on the way, and I fully believe that you can too.

When thinking about your career success at this time of your life, it is fundamental that you fully understand what the key strategic goals of your organisation are. They may change from time to time, so make sure that you are up to speed. Spend some time working through how your role can make a positive impact on those goals. For example, if you work within HR and a key goal of the business is creating new services to help boost revenue, can you support this by working on a plan that ensures the business has the right talent and/or skills to create this new service division? Make sure that your plan is in line with or even improves on any revenue projections they have. Ensuring that your day-to-day achievements and tasks are closely aligned with the business's goals will help you build a successful career and will also build a strong case for your advancement.

Before we get into the details, I will add that if you are unable to physically carry out your role, then do speak with your employer, as they have an obligation to do a risk assessment to find suitable alternatives.

Visibility

Don't go missing in the virtual or physical workplace when you are pregnant! Visibility is key. It may be tempting to shrink into the background as you head towards such a big life change, but don't give into the temptation.

You have to be strategic and intentional with how you show up. Regular office drinks every week may be difficult, but think about attending key social events that allow you to be present and build important relationships. If key people aren't aware of you, you'll probably miss out on opportunities to improve your skills and take on interesting assignments, despite your hard work and good performance while being pregnant. Being visible is so important, because sadly we know that from time to time, discrimination in the workplace happens to pregnant women. Visibility helps to keep you at the front of people's minds for opportunities. This is especially important if you work remotely, and while you're on maternity leave, because people might forget about you if they don't often see you in person.

How to boost your visibility when pregnant

Plan ahead for your meetings. Think about your role in the meeting ahead of time. What impact do you want to make? Be ready to listen to others and share helpful ideas. Before you contribute to the meeting, make sure your comment is really going to add value. Speak up when you have something important to be shared; don't shrink yourself.

Attend socials. These are still important. You will be tired and many times you won't feel like going, but pick out the few in the calendar that you think will be beneficial, and be open to building new and stronger connections with people.

Get involved in strategic projects. Are there any key projects that help the business reach its strategic objectives where you can add value? If so, consider getting involved. If there aren't any obvious opportunities, then let your manager know that if such projects arise, you want to be involved, irrespective of being pregnant.

Invest in building your network relentlessly

This is so important to do – before, during and after your maternity leave. Build your network outside of your office also. It's rare that advancement is down to luck or just performance alone. It's more likely to be due to hard work and knowing the right people.

Aim for regular coffee meetings (these could be virtual) with people who could help advance your career, now or in the future. Don't just ask to pick their brains; that is unlikely to get you far. Be specific about why you would like to meet, and think about how you can benefit them in return.

Don't be afraid to reach out to people who you generally admire on LinkedIn. I've done this on both of my maternity leaves, and I've made some amazing connections who have encouraged me and helped me in my personal and professional life. It feels daunting at first, but give it a try!

Don't go into these interactions just thinking about what you can get from them. Think about helping others as much as you can. People always remember those who have helped them. The most effective way of doing this can be connecting people to the right people who can help. Try to close every interaction with others by asking, 'Is there anything I can do to help you?'

Find a mentor and a sponsor

Let's just touch upon the difference between the two. A mentor gives advice and guides you throughout your career. A sponsor is your advocate; they have a seat at the table, and will be able to speak positively on your behalf when key decisions are being made.

In terms of finding a mentor, a great fit would be someone who gets your role or your industry and what it takes to succeed. And for a sponsor, you want to seek out someone who sits on the board or executive committee of your organisation. Ideally, it should be someone with whom you have mutual interests, and whom you can also support in terms of furthering any initiatives they are working on with your organisation. Your performance has to be stellar to secure a sponsor; they are putting themselves on the line to support you, so make sure they are aware of your great work.

Why is it important to have both a mentor and a sponsor?

When you are pregnant, you will need BOTH a mentor and a sponsor more than ever.

You need a mentor because you will have difficult days and you need someone to advise you through them who understands your role and what you are trying to achieve. Based on their own experience, a mentor can also advise you on how to tackle certain situations that you may have to work through in your professional and personal lives.

A sponsor is mission-critical, especially if you are looking to progress. There are several studies that prove that a sponsor is key to helping people fast-track their careers. You need someone who can influence those key decisions around pay and promotion, and who can champion you and put your name forward for opportunities. We know it is wrong to discriminate against pregnant women when it comes to career opportunities, but we also know that from time to time, it happens. There may be some old-school naysayers who believe a pregnant woman cannot be productive or shouldn't be promoted. So I wholeheartedly believe you need a sponsor who will fight extra hard for you. This becomes even more important when you are on maternity leave and are not there to advocate for yourself. It's a good idea that your sponsor is also included in your handover process.

Make life easy for your sponsor. They are likely to be in an incredibly demanding senior role, so before you go on maternity leave, I would prepare a document listing your key achievements over the last twelve months, with supporting evidence, so that if any relevant opportunities for advancement come up while you are pregnant or on maternity leave, then they have all the data easily available and they can convincingly put you forward.

Socialise your goals

Once you have a mentor and a sponsor, make sure that they are both aware of your career goals, and that you make a plan to keep in touch with them while on maternity leave. Do not internalise your goals just because you are pregnant; communicate them to your mentor and sponsor, and together agree a plan of what needs to be done to achieve them.

Put in the work

Put in the work and make sure your achievements are visible. In a few months, you'll be out of the office. So now is the time to leave a lasting impression that you are both dependable and committed. It is about focusing on the tasks that add value, and not just doing everything for the sake of looking good, because you will soon burn out doing so – especially while pregnant.

As you put in the work, document your achievements and communicate them using language that tells a story of business success as well as the part that you played too.

Can you be promoted when you are pregnant?

Absolutely – it is happening more and more! Deborah Ajaja's story is incredibly inspiring, and is a brilliant example of lots of the strategies in this book being put into action and paying off.

Words of wisdom from Deborah Ajaja

Deborah is a former senior operations leader at a global tech company, and she is also the mother of two beautiful young children. In 2019, when Deborah was expecting her second child and working for one of the Big Four consultancies, she was promoted to the head of her division.

I was considering going for a promotion well before it even became a viable option, and this was around the time of my first maternity leave. So, when I came back, I was laser-focused. I knew what the task at hand was. I saw my path to a promotion during my pregnancy as consisting of a few key steps. Firstly, I made sure to understand the exact criteria needed to secure that promotion. I spent a lot of time studying the role, what was required, the soft skills, the development skills, the delivery skills, the management skills, to then be able to evidence I was ready for it.

The second thing, which I think is probably the most important, was to find a sponsor, and I was incredibly fortunate in that I'd been working with senior management for a long time, and I had a strong relationship with one of the Partners. She was not my direct manager, but was massively influential. I was clear and upfront with her about my desire to achieve a promotion and the time frame I wanted to do it in. Because sponsorship works on a quid pro quo basis, I was very clear about what I needed from her and also what I'd give her in return.

Thirdly, I was incredibly loud and unapologetic about what I was going for. Every time I had a meeting with my line manager, I would refer back to my promotion goals, my achievements in that current week, and reiterate the time frame we were working with to ensure that we were aligned. I did it in every single meeting – it was almost embarrassing! – and each time I would come prepared with a checklist. I would say things like, 'This is what I've done since the last time we discussed it, this is the additional endorsement I've received, this is how I've evidenced this particular skill set. This is what shows I'm ready for this role.' I think by doing this consistently, I was reminding and showing him how serious and robustly equipped I was.

It also served as a source of self-affirmation, reminding me that I was on track and perfectly capable.

During that process, I later found out I was pregnant. Fantastic news; unexpected, but still a brilliant milestone for me and my family. But because of the groundwork that had already been laid, it didn't stop anything. I spoke to my line manager and my sponsor about the pregnancy, and they assured me that it wouldn't change the plan. If anything, it meant that the time frame became a bit more aggressive.

My sponsor took me aside and said that they were going to demand a lot of me if I was to secure the promotion, and asked me if I was ready for it. I knew that she was rooting for me every step of the way, but she wanted me to be clear on exactly what it would take to get there, and ensure that I was fully committed to putting in the effort irrespective of being pregnant. I was all in, and so we had an explicit agreement. I was aware of what it would take, given the slight change in my circumstances, but I was resolved. I knew that while I was physically evolving and developing and growing this wonderful new human being, mentally, professionally, emotionally, I was all there. I was ready.

We carried on with the process, and continued with everything that was required to secure that promotion. It just so happened that there was a two-month gap between the promotion cycle ending and when I was due to go on maternity leave. So, the dates worked out well and I secured the promotion! Thankfully,

I have a really great story to tell, one which I'm always happy to share to hopefully help others.

It's so important to have the self-belief and confidence that you can actually do it. And the reason I say that is because for you to even be in a position where you can be considered or put yourself forward for promotion, you'll have some track record sitting in your back pocket, right? You've already delivered something, you've proven your worth, you will have shown great potential – key indicators for your readiness to take things to the next level. Whether or not you're pregnant is neither here nor there, and it takes absolutely nothing away from the fact that you can deliver in that elevated role. And whether you start that role immediately or after a maternity leave, shouldn't make a difference. I would absolutely encourage you to believe in yourself and to put everything you can ahead of you to secure that promotion. You can do it.

Prepare for your return before you go on maternity leave

This is so incredibly important. Why? Because for the first few months after your precious little one arrives, you will be completely absorbed by your new role as a mum to this new baby. You need to set the foundations before your life changes in a big way. If you haven't done so already, don't be scared – this advice is not being shared to make you feel anxious, it is to equip you to make a start.

How to prepare for your return before you go on maternity leave

Here are some of the things to start thinking about and preparing for:

Childcare

As soon as you've had your twelve-week scan, start thinking about the different childcare options available to you – for example, nanny, childminder, nursery or family help. There's more on this in Chapter 6. Find out about the cost for different configurations, such as a full week versus three days, and work through which option may suit you best. Chapter 2 shares lots of information on the financial help available from the government, and you can ask your workplace if they offer any additional help with childcare costs, too.

Do you need flexibility?

It's a big question to ask before the baby has arrived. But start to think about what flexibility you may need, if at all. Have this chat with your partner too (if that is applicable), to establish what flexibility you both need and what options he or she has to help make things work.

You don't need to have a chat with work straight away, but do start to think about the benefits of the options that suit you best. It will help you to build a compelling business case.

Your network

Your network will be invaluable to you during your leave and upon your return. It can help you to settle back into the organisation quickly, or to pivot or find your next opportunity.

Assess your network where it is weak and where it is strong. Perhaps where it is weak, use this time to think about how to strengthen it. You could use this time to connect with women in your industry who have had a successful return and find out how they did it.

Work on your confidence

This is the most common challenge I hear from women regarding their return. A lot will change over the coming months, and being physically away from work can make you feel like you've forgotten what you know. Before you go on maternity leave, write down all the achievements that you are proud of, and in those moments of doubt read them back to yourself to remind yourself of how capable you are and train your brain to overcome the negative thoughts. More on confidence in Chapter 8.

Think about your skill gaps

Do you have any skill gaps you need to fill? Can you find an opportunity to fill some of those gaps on maternity leave or soon after? This is a tough one, because finding time is very difficult. You may be lucky enough to identify what skills gaps you have, and then you can start to think about how you want to close them, which is a positive start. But you may not have the time to really work on this until after maternity leave. I remember wanting to level up on my Excel skills during my maternity leave, and it never happened. However, I did learn lots of other things, largely via Google and YouTube, that helped me to work on the skills gaps I had in other areas.

Vocalise your ambitions

Make sure before you go on maternity leave that your boss and your sponsor (if you have one) know about your ambitions, so that if any relevant opportunities crop up while you are on maternity leave, you are considered. If it's really important to you, don't be afraid to share how you would like to be contacted if anything relevant to your ambitions opens up.

Look into the future

What do you think your life might look like with a child?

It might mean a new house with more space, or rethinking how you do business travel. It is great to get ahead of all the things that could possibly change, and to think about how those things may impact your day-to-day life at work, and what kind of solutions you might consider.

Chapter 4
Planning a successful maternity leave

In this chapter, I will guide you through how to decide on the length of your maternity leave, and how you can plan a successful maternity leave. I'll also share the experience of an amazing couple who have taken shared parental leave three times.

When I think about my two maternity leave experiences, they bring back a wave of different feelings and emotions. Honestly, during my first maternity leave, I was all over the place emotionally! I thought that, having come from a huge family and been around lots of children growing up, my maternity leave would be a breeze. Plus, I was on this journey with my fabulous crew of yummy mummies of 2017, the group of friends who were all having babies at the same time as me. I was so wrong.

This was my first dive into motherhood, and I spent most of my maternity leave trying to figure out what the hell was happening to me and my life. I thought as soon as I had the baby, I would just hop out of my hospital bed and be back to my normal, active self. I think I tried to go for a walk seventy-two hours after giving birth, and after ten minutes, I felt like my insides might fall out and had to hobble back home. I was baffled by so many things, like how I could get the baby to sleep at night so that I could find a moment to recuperate. I actually threw away all of my maternity clothes the night before I was induced, because I thought I no longer needed them! I now know that was a stupid thing to do, as maternity jeans have a firm place in your life long after your baby arrives. I remember watching a YouTube video in the middle of the Westfield car park to help me take the car seat off the buggy, as I had no idea how to get the baby back in the car. My mum moved in with us for almost two weeks to help us with the new baby, and when she announced she was going back to her house, I wept! I had no idea how I was going to cope without her. The first six months were spent trying to reconcile why I felt I had 'lost' my old life; in many ways, I think I was grieving my old life a little bit. I was trying to figure out how I could still do and experience the things I had deeply loved before I had a child, trying to figure out if I had changed or was still the same person, and trying to keep a small child alive and healthy – all on very little sleep. I can't say that I enjoyed those first six months. It wasn't the 'break' that lots of people think it is. It was a huge life change, perhaps one of the biggest I think anyone can ever experience.

I say all of this because maternity leave is such a special time, but it can also be a very complicated time filled with heaps of change. So I think you have to give yourself some time to adjust and bond with your baby. Which is why I strongly believe in laying the groundwork with your career as much as possible *before* going on maternity leave, because as soon as the baby arrives, you will be consumed with figuring things out – and rightly so.

I've learned so much from both of my maternity leaves, and so I want to share as much as I possibly can with you so that you feel empowered and confident about your career and taking time off to look after your little one.

Deciding on the length of your maternity leave

There are so many factors to consider when making the decision of how much time to take for maternity leave, money being a huge one. Before we have a look at the financial side of things, let's look at the length of time you can take off on leave, and balancing that with your career. I know it's something lots of women worry about. We worry that being off for a long time can potentially hurt our careers and mean that we might miss out on opportunities. So I am going to break down all the key things to consider to help you make the best decision for you.

The length of your maternity leave has an impact on the role you may come back to

Something you may not know is that the length of time you take off can impact the exact role you will return to. If you take six months or less, then the organisation must keep your job exactly as it was for you to return to. If you take more than six months, you have the right to return to the same role unless it is no longer available, in which case they must give you a similar job with the same pay and conditions.

There can be loads of changes at work in the time that you're off; you only have to look at the world around us to know this to be true. For example, the business could be forced to go through a restructure because of a pandemic and subsequent changes to the economy. So, if you are planning to be off for more than six months, be mindful that you may be offered a different role upon your return. It's not something to worry about, as the role you are offered must at the very least have the same terms and conditions as your old one. You may even find that the new role offered to you is better. It's another reason why it's so important to vocalise your ambitions and your achievements before you go on maternity leave, so that when decisions around the role you are coming back to are made, they are in line with what you would love to do and what you're good at.

If you're not happy with the role they have offered you, then I would encourage you not to be afraid to discuss it. Everything is up for negotiation, and there may be different ways in which the role could be moulded that would work well for the business – and for you, too. In these discussions, talk about your strengths and achievements, and how these will help propel the business forward.

If you want to take more than six months of maternity leave, then please don't let this put you off. It is one of those bits of the law that is in place to protect you and give your employer a bit of flexibility while protecting your terms of employment.

How long can you take for maternity leave?

In the UK, you have the right to take up to a year, and you have the right to not tell your employer when you would like to return until eight weeks before. I've mentioned before that I don't recommend leaving this all up to chance and waiting until the last minute to let your boss know when you are coming back. So I recommend giving a rough indication of how long you would like to take, making it clear that you will let work know if anything changes. The reality is you really do have to hold your space and proactively protect your career, even when on maternity leave. It is totally possible to do so when you are ready by using your keeping in touch (KIT) days, networking and being proactive.

Can a long maternity leave hurt your career?

The research says it can, but you can certainly limit the impact, and this impact can be very minimal if you actively manage your time away.

Research from 2018 in Canada, where maternity leave is similar to the UK and can be up to twelve months, shows that a longer maternity leave can have a negative impact on the perceptions of a woman and her commitment to her career.[13] I hate this assertion, but it is what the research says. The study also goes on to show that where the woman has the ability to keep in touch with the business, she is able to mitigate those perceptions of commitment and hireability. Interestingly, in the same study, when there was information given about the women on maternity leave, specifically a letter from her boss that detailed her career ambitions and work habits, there was no negative impact on how she was perceived and her hireability.

What this study does show is why it is so important to do all that you reasonably can to proactively manage your career before, during and after your maternity leave if you are thinking of taking close to twelve months. There is also no harm in being intentional about your career even if you plan to take a shorter break.

Deep down, I know that so many women who go on maternity leave completely bust this notion of being less committed. The chances are, if you are reading this book, you are highly committed and motivated, and want to push ahead in your career. What makes it difficult is people sometimes holding outdated conceptions. It is sad but true that we have to work twice as hard or be twice as intentional to have the same opportunities as our colleagues who aren't taking time off to have children.

What can you do to mitigate the impact of a long maternity leave?

Take advantage of your keeping in touch days

I think it is a missed opportunity not to use any keeping in touch days. Even if you use just one, please try your very best to do so. It's a great idea to chat with your boss beforehand and discuss the different ways in which it would be beneficial to use your keeping in touch days. I found it really helpful to spend a day with colleagues running through updates and current projects to get a sense of big changes at work and what it looked like in terms of the day-to-day work. With more and more of us working remotely I think it's become even easier to make use of KIT days. On my second maternity leave, I broke my days up into chunks so I arranged meetings during nap times which helped massively as I didn't have to arrange childcare. Don't be afraid to use your KIT days to remind people of the value that you bring to the table.

Share your achievements widely

As we have seen in the research, the perception of women taking a long maternity leave was maintained if there were facts to support their ambition and working habits. It drives home why it is critical to be your own cheerleader and shout about your own achievements. You could do this when you are sharing your handover: you could summarise key projects that you have been involved with in the last twelve months and the achievements based on your actions, so that anyone who has access to your handover also has access to your achievements.

If you manage someone going on maternity leave, then one of the most powerful things you can do is send an email to key stakeholders in the businesses that shares details of the maternity cover plan, but that also raves about the brilliant achievements of the person going on maternity leave.

Talk about your return positively

You will have all kinds of feelings about your return, and that is perfectly okay to admit – and it's also perfectly okay to share your apprehensions. But I would also always include what you are looking forward to about coming back to work. It reminds people about the enthusiasm that you have for your role and for achieving your goals.

Communicate how you would like to be contacted

Some women want to completely disconnect during their maternity leave. I do think there are advantages to staying lightly connected: it keeps you visible and front of mind. It is totally up to you to define how you want this to work. It could be that you want work to keep you in the loop with office-wide updates that impact everyone. Alternatively, it could be that you want to join certain company-wide virtual meetings (with your camera off), and you can use your KIT days for this.

Consider shared parental leave

If your partner is willing and able, shared parental leave could be a brilliant way to help mitigate any negative impact of a long maternity leave. Shared parental leave has a ridiculously low uptake of 2%. I still think this is largely down to earning discrepancies between men and women. Because men on the whole earn significantly more than women, losing the largest part of your household income just isn't feasible for some families, so I get it. Some companies have an incredibly attractive shared parental leave policy, so it is always worth your partner checking their policy to see what is on offer. Some companies offer men six months' full pay that can be taken during the first five years of the child's life. If you can make the finances work, this has incredible benefits. It might even be worth getting your partner to have a read of the experience of Ruki and John below if they are hesitant about shared parental leave.

Words of wisdom from John and Ruki

Ruki and John are a couple for whom I have a lot of respect. They have experienced shared parental leave three times while both working in the world of finance. Here, they share their experience and the impact it's had on their parenting and their careers, which I am so grateful for, as it is rare that we get to hear these perspectives, especially that of a father taking leave.

John

We elected to do shared parental leave more or less as soon as we knew that it was an option, and we are currently experiencing shared parental leave for the third time. We did it with our first son Grayson soon after the legislation came into place. I discovered that I was one of the first people in my company to ever take it. So, it was very new ground for everybody. There were a lot of confusing conversations with both HR and my team as I was gearing up to it. What I discovered quite quickly was that in my company, despite the fact they have a reasonably generous maternity policy, the policy for dads taking parental leave was the opposite; it was the legal minimum that they had to give. So, there was no pay other than statutory rate, and no kind of structural provisions. For example, things like keeping in touch days are well established within the maternity leave framework, but it just wasn't something that was very well understood for shared parental leave. I remember having a lot of very interesting conversations leading up to it. Being an American firm, I think there's always a slight reluctance to accept or understand the idea of taking any time off. I think that's both for men and women, because in America the situation is a lot more constrained. Interestingly, I did get a lot of kind comments, particularly from older guys in the team, more senior guys saying that they wished that they had been able to do that when they had their children. And so I took some comfort from that, and it helped me to feel like I was making the right decision. Whether it was convenient to the business, and I know it wasn't, I felt secure in what I was doing. However, because of the less-than-generous pay situation, I ended up only taking one month of shared parental leave and one month of paid holiday, in order to not have that impact us quite so significantly. We'd only just moved and bought our first house, we had a nursery deposit to pay, and I was the main breadwinner, taking time off and not being paid for all of that time. We had to try and figure out a way to make it work financially. Essentially, I was unpaid for only one month out of the two months, which lessened the impact a bit.

In terms of the experience of shared parental leave, it was the best thing ever, and I felt really lucky to have had that time with Grayson, because I was taking over at a time when Grayson was *getting really interesting as a baby; he was starting to build a personality and he was just about to start walking. So, it was great! We had little outings and we'd go to the shops and have lunch together, and he became like my mate, basically. It was really, really, really, really wonderful. And obviously Ruki was going back to work, so I'll let her share her perspective.*

Ruki

Stepping back. Someone had mentioned shared parental leave to me when I was pregnant. And it sounded amazing, because it helps to level out the playing field again. I had typically always seen women be the primary caregivers and all the great stuff associated with that, but also the difficult stuff associated with that. I remember going to the hairdresser before I had kids and seeing a woman sitting under the dryer. Her phone rang and she answered it to her partner or husband saying that the children were crying and wouldn't settle, and he didn't know where things were, and he told the lady that she needed to come home. And so she left, even though she was halfway through getting her hair done.

This really resonated with me. It was years before I came to have kids, but I remember thinking, gosh, how difficult must it be to try and live your life again when you have kids if you're constantly being pulled back into that motherhood role, and have the responsibility of being the only one who can do something. Even at work, you're not the only person who can do something; you share tasks amongst your colleagues. And so I knew I had to find a way to do that at home. When I found out about shared parental leave, this was very much part of my proposition to John. I said to him that if we were going to go into the world of parenting, we were going to share the load. I remember thinking financially it would be difficult for us as a family. But this thought has always stayed with me that no amount of money can buy that time back, and that's always been our thinking, each time that we've shared parental leave. No matter what happens financially, and obviously that is something to consider, we both agreed that the time you get with your child in those early months is precious time that you only get once.

In terms of how I found it going back to work, it was amazing, because I didn't really have any worries. I didn't have to worry about the nursery calling about a sick child or my son not settling in. I got to go back to work and almost switch off from parenting mode and focus on being back at work. Knowing that my child was in the best care possible gave me that freedom to really throw myself into work. Additionally, I remember that I'd been at home for ten months, running the ship effectively my way, which I thought was the best way. What I found is that even though we had maybe two or three days of handover, John found his own way of doing things and it worked. So that has always stuck with me: that John does his things his way, and that is totally fine.

John

As a guy, one of the best things about parental leave is that you get a real, honest appreciation of what it's like for mums on maternity leave. I think we often have a very skewed picture of what we think it's like. I don't consider myself to be particularly insensitive. But I remember honestly my mind going to that place of wondering what Ruki had done all day when she handed the baby over to me as soon as I'd come back home from a long day in the office. It felt like I was having to start another working day. Well, I did feel like that, until I was on parental leave, and I recognised that when you're with the baby all day and your wife's at work, being at home with a little one is ten times harder than being in the office.

You have a greater sense of appreciation, and it enhanced my respect for my wife, because Ruki had done it for a long time, and during an even harder stage of raising a baby. So, you feel like you understand what childcare is all about, and what it means to look after a baby essentially on your own during the day, without much respite. It was nice to have the playing field levelled out.

Shared parental leave allows mums to hit the ground running when they go back to work, without having to deal with the guilt that may come from leaving your little one with strangers. Interestingly, from my perspective, when I went back after a relatively short period of time, just a couple of months, I didn't feel particularly disadvantaged going back. I had not been especially diligent at staying in touch because it was only two months, and, candidly, I just had more important things to do, but I think because I had all of the difficult and slightly awkward conversations ahead of time, everyone was sort of on the right page when I left. I managed my handover pretty well, and so it wasn't particularly challenging going back. In fact, the only real challenge, I think, was the guilt that perhaps a mother might ordinarily have going back after maternity leave. I was probably having a bit of that guilt because I had handed him over to the nursery and was wondering how it was all going.

The first parental leave and second parental leave were probably quite consistent with each other. Zach, our second, was younger when I took over. It was largely the same, but it was a bit less fun dealing with an eight-month-old as opposed to a ten-month-old, but it was also good. The third time round is a bit unusual as I've moved firms. I'm now at a UK bank, and they have a much more enlightened policy when it comes to parental leave. Essentially, they treat mums and dads the same, and so I'm able to take up to about five months off, fully paid, which is amazing. Once I had managed to figure out what the policy was and how it all works, which is easier said than done (and pretty much the case in every company), I signalled that I wanted to take parental leave and it was very much like, go for it. There wasn't any pushback, which I'll be eternally grateful for, because it's given me a really good chunk of time to spend with Ruben, and

I've really been able to get stuck in – which can be pretty messy, but it's ultimately infinitely rewarding. I haven't gone back to work yet, so it remains to be seen what the impact of this time off will be. Hopefully it'll be relatively seamless.

Ruki

To anyone who is thinking of taking shared parental leave, I would echo what I said earlier, which is that you can't get the time back. As a parent, there are so many chapters that everybody agrees just fly by so quickly, and this is one of them. The sleepless nights go quickly, the teething goes quickly, the maternity and then the shared parental leave goes so quickly as well. It's a memory that you will have forever, and I really think it makes you a well-rounded parent. As a mum, going back to work and leaving your partner at home with the baby, you feel better because there's less pressure on you, and you know you're releasing some of the control that you might have had. That makes you a better parent, because you're less of a control freak and it also forces the dad to figure things out. Then, when you both become working parents and you've got that time on the weekend, you're both more efficient as parents as you don't rely on one person to carry the burden. If I could sum it up, I say the time is precious, so just go for it.

John

I have two pieces of advice. The first is a practical one for dads or potential dads considering shared parental leave with their partner. Treat it in the way that you would expect your partner to treat maternity leave, which is to say, do the due diligence upfront, go through the policy language with a fine-tooth comb, speak to HR, speak to your line manager, have those conversations in detail – or in as much detail as you can – and understand the terms. Understand what you are entitled to, what you're not entitled to, as it's easy to trip up due to lack of understanding. Treat the organisation with respect in terms of handovers and make sure that you're not leaving them in the lurch, because you will create a lot of goodwill around your leave if you do it well. Not to mention in many cases, you'll be setting a precedent for other dads and partners who might want to follow in your footsteps, and you want to make sure you're leaving a good taste in your employer's mouth when you do it.

The other thing I would say is don't expect that you'll have a lot of free time on parental leave. I made the mistake of imagining all the extracurricular things I might be able to do when I'm off work, and I've done about 1%, because there just isn't that much time. But the time I've spent with the kids has been more than enough to make it fulfilling. I just don't think you're going to improve your golf handicap in that time as well.

The balance equation

So, once you have weighed up the impact of the length of your maternity leave on your career and goals, think about the optimal time you would like to take. Secondly, overlap this with your finances. Use financial planning tools to help with this. On the My Bump Pay website within the free resources, you can find a Maternity Leave Budget sheet, which can help you plan how long you can afford to take. I have included the link in the Notes section of this book. This will help you in deciding what is the optimal amount of time to have off as maternity leave.

With my first maternity leave, I took twelve months, plus an additional four weeks of annual leave, so in total I was away from work for thirteen months. This was the time I felt that I needed for so many reasons. I found the first six months of maternity leave really challenging. By the time I got into my parenting groove, I felt like I wanted more time to really master motherhood and rediscover myself and the things I love. Hence, I took more than twelve months off. This time also birthed My Bump Pay, so I don't have a lot of regrets about the amount I took. For my second maternity leave I took ten months, which felt perfect for me the second time around.

What is the best way to let your manager know how long you would like to take for maternity leave?

This is one of those conversations that no one really tells you how to navigate. For some, it's quite a straightforward conversation, because you may feel incredibly supported by your manager and your colleagues as you journey through your pregnancy. For others, it may feel like yet another daunting conversation to have if you are the first person in your office to go on maternity leave, like I was, or maybe because other mums at your company tend to come back to work after a really short leave and you want to experience a longer maternity leave. Maybe you feel anxious about stepping away from your role and nervous that your replacement may make it difficult for you to settle back in. So for many reasons, this conversation can be difficult.

Remember you don't legally have to confirm when you are returning to work until eight weeks before you intend to go back. However, I think being proactive and giving some kind of indication is helpful and shows you are willing to cooperate.

Here is an example of how you could phrase it in either a conversation or an email. You can take out what isn't relevant to you.

'My due date is _____. I would like my last working day in the office to be ____. Combined with the use of ___holiday days, my maternity leave will begin on ____. I anticipate taking leave of _____ months.

If anything changes, I will be sure to let you know as soon as possible, because pregnancy and parenthood can be unpredictable. Thank you for allowing me to have this time away from the office to look after the new baby. Closer to the time, I will work to create a detailed plan of my activities and responsibilities to provide as smooth a handover as possible. If there is anything that you would like for me to consider in this plan, do let me know. I will be on hand as always for any questions on my personal mobile during my leave, and I hope to do a few keeping in touch days, but do keep me in the loop regarding any key changes.'

Maternity leave doesn't mean your career is over

There are a lot of horror stories about women's careers and maternity leave. It's awful what some companies get away with when it comes to discrimination against pregnant women. We can't ignore that it happens, and if you think that you are being treated differently because you are pregnant, then I would always advise seeking further support from a solicitor, ACAS or the Pregnant Then Screwed helpline. It must be noted that not all companies treat expectant women unfairly. There are lots of brilliant companies doing wonderful things for women.

I do believe that a big part of maternity leave is going into it with the right mindset – aka the maternity mindset. How we see maternity leave needs to be reset, because from this life-changing time can come the most wonderful opportunity for personal development.

So, how do you adopt this maternity leave mindset?

1. Take time to think about what you really want

Figuring this out does take time. Maternity leave can be a brilliant opportunity to be ruthlessly honest with yourself about the life that you want to create for you and your family. See that as a real benefit; there are not many times in life we get to ponder our values. Our values shape us and can be a powerful North Star as we start to walk down the road of working parenthood.

2. Remind yourself often that you are raising the next generation

Under an ever-mounting load of laundry, this can easily be forgotten. Raising children is actually one of the hardest things I have ever done. Yet very few things have such a lasting and tangible impact on the world we live in than shaping and raising a new generation.

3. Look after yourself

Your wellbeing will impact your mindset and how you see things, and so checking in with yourself to make sure you are genuinely okay is important. Maternity leave is intense, and looking after yourself is just as important as looking after your baby. Try to incorporate some time alone into your maternity leave, or time to do the things that you love and that help you to recharge.

4. Don't make the journey alone

You don't have to do maternity leave all by yourself. It can be incredibly lonely at times, so it's so important that you find people to make the journey with. Don't be afraid to share your ups, downs and also your ambitions with them. Talking about the things that you love and finding like-minded people to share the experience with is a massive encouragement to stay true to yourself. During my first maternity leave, I had an amazing group of women who were so supportive. We cried and laughed together, as well as cheering each other on when someone shared a goal or hit an important milestone.

How to boost your career on maternity leave

Before I became a mum, I never thought that this could ever happen. Maybe it's because we've been fed the narrative that a woman's career is finished the moment she begins the journey of motherhood, without ever being shown the other side of the story – the stories of women who have smashed the stereotypes.

I feel at this point I have to include two important caveats.

The first is that maternity leave is FAR from easy. I would hate to make this sound like, oh, you just have to follow seven magical steps to success to have a career-enhancing maternity leave. That would be so incredibly irresponsible of me. You may find that maternity leave is all-consuming and therefore the time for any of this other stuff is limited. That is okay!

Secondly, you may do all these steps and find things in your career don't work out the way that you'd hoped while on maternity leave, due to things that are completely out of your control. That is okay too. It could be because the timing doesn't line up with things in your organisation, or you may be working in an environment which doesn't have progressive attitudes towards women on maternity leave.

I guess what I am trying to say is that a) how you spend your maternity leave is deeply personal and unique to you, and b) focus on the things that you can control.

So here are a few tips that can help boost your career while on maternity leave.

Try not to go missing on maternity leave

It's tempting to completely disappear off the work radar on maternity leave, and it's so easy to do. But your visibility is still important. A number of career-impacting decisions are happening all the time. From my experience on leadership teams, companies are constantly thinking about their growth and how to achieve that growth, which is often delivered through their people. So, as companies think about which people they need to play a key role in helping them achieve their next level of growth, you need to remain relevant in their considerations and conversations. I've talked previously about why KIT days are brilliant, so if possible do try to make use of them as a way of staying visible while on maternity leave.

Use maternity leave to your advantage

Taking time away from work gives you an opportunity to see your organisation from a completely different perspective. It's not an opportunity that many people get, so it's something you can definitely use to your advantage. It may allow you to come up with new proposals that help improve things where you work, or it may even spark ideas that help you develop personally. My whole platform was birthed while on maternity leave, which felt like crazy timing but it's one of the best things that has happened to me.

Make sure you are still involved in any formal performance reviews

Many companies have formal review or promotion cycles. These may fall while you are on maternity leave, and that is okay. If you don't know when these reviews happen, then definitely ask before you go on maternity leave. If you can agree between yourself and your boss, you can use a KIT day to be present for your performance review. Go prepared! Be as prepared as you would be for a board meeting or interview. Have all your facts and figures to hand to support your achievements. If you can't be present, then I would put together a document that evidences all of your relevant achievements, and make sure that your boss and/or sponsor has a copy of this. As a side note, when you are on maternity leave, you should absolutely be considered a part of any salary or performance review that is happening. You should not be left out because you are on leave. It doesn't mean that you have to be physically present, but it does mean that you must be considered in the same way as any other member of staff.

Invest in your network

This isn't as daunting as it sounds. I see networking as keeping in touch with people with whom you have come into contact during your personal and professional career. I think these relationships should be reciprocal, and you shouldn't just contact people when you need something. It really won't get you very far. So on maternity leave, I would, where possible, reach out to people within your network to check in and see how they are or stay in the loop. You can also engage with them via LinkedIn.

Chapter 5

Freelancers and founders – building a business and a family

I think there is a cohort of women who are massively underserved when it comes to information on the topic of working parenthood. You can probably guess by the title of this chapter which group this is: women who are self-employed or founders. I hope that I can shed some light on how different women have approached it. So, this chapter will cover maternity pay for those who are self-employed or a founder, maternity leave, building a side hustle while on maternity leave, and words of wisdom from Georgie Coleridge Cole, the editor and founder of Sheerluxe, as well as Alexandra Stedman, founder of The Frugality.

Maternity pay if you are self-employed

So, let's break down how to navigate maternity pay if you are self-employed as simply as possible.

Maternity allowance

If you are fully self-employed and have no other income, you may be eligible for maternity allowance (MA), which is a government benefit specifically for expectant mothers who aren't eligible for statutory maternity pay (which is what you would typically get if you were employed).

You can claim maternity allowance from twenty-six weeks pregnant and onwards. The earliest that payments can start is eleven weeks before your baby is due.

You can get between £27 and £156.66 a week for thirty-nine weeks if you're self-employed. This amount is likely to increase slightly from April 2023.

To help you get the maximum amount of money, you need to make sure you are paying your Class 2 National Insurance contributions before your baby is due. If you pay as many contributions as possible in the sixty-six weeks before your baby is due this will help you get the maximum amount of maternity allowance.

How do you know if you qualify for maternity allowance?

In the sixty-six weeks before your baby is born, you need to:

- have been registered as self-employed for twenty-six weeks
- have earned £30 or more for thirteen weeks (the thirteen weeks do not need to be continuous)

The government has a super-handy calculator which you can use to see if you are eligible: www.gov.uk/maternity-paternity-pay-leave

What happens if tragically you lose the baby?

- If baby loss happens after twenty-four weeks, you may still qualify for maternity allowance, if you meet the qualifying conditions.
- If the baby is born alive at any point during the pregnancy, you may also be eligible.

Don't delay

I've spoken to a number of women who have experienced lengthy delays when it comes to maternity allowance, which can cause a huge amount of worry and stress that you simply do not need. The process is not the easiest, so give yourself time, and please don't leave it to the very last minute to fill out all the forms.

Get help if you can

If you have an accountant, then definitely get their help to make sure you have all the information you need for a super-smooth application. They can also advise you on how to structure your freelance or business income to help you financially prepare for the time that you are going to take off. It might feel odd to talk to your accountant about plans to expand your family, but the advice of a good accountant in these scenarios can be invaluable to help you plan your way through this time. A seasoned accountant will likely have experience with all types of business owners and their maternity pay, and so will be able to advise you best, based on your personal circumstances.

Maternity pay for a founder

If you run a business and pay yourself via the payroll of your business, then you should qualify for statutory maternity pay as long as you meet the criteria for it explained in Chapter 2.

If you don't meet the criteria for statutory maternity pay, then you would have to go ahead and start the process for maternity allowance.

Words of wisdom from Alexandra Stedman

I've loved following Alexandra's journey building her business, the lifestyle hub The Frugality. On her platform, she speaks very openly about money, and she was incredibly gracious in sharing her experience of navigating her finances as a freelancer and a founder on maternity leave.

Planning for pregnancy and maternity is an amazing thing on paper, but there is never really a good time to have a baby. Obviously, a little planning and having a bit of money behind you helps that transition. But financially, especially the first time, it can be difficult, as you don't know what to expect until you've experienced it.

I planned to have three weeks off with my first baby. I don't know why, because I didn't have any childcare in place. I just pulled that number out of the air. I knew I was going to have a baby, but I was still very focused on work. My thinking was that I couldn't be away from work for much longer than three weeks, because my job requires me to do things daily; that's the nature of the beast with social media. It's not easy at all, it's so all-consuming, and you're also navigating the loss of freedom as a new mother. There are lots of other things as well as work to find your way through: there's your loss of self, you're not in charge of your own body. So you can plan, but you might find a lot of it goes out of the window.

Financially, maternity leave as a freelancer can be tricky. You get maternity allowance, which works out at approximately £150 a week, which is the most you can take. What I didn't take into consideration was the fact that I work with my husband, and if you're with a male freelance partner, they don't claim any paternity. Which I think is crazy, because he looks after our child as well. It's hard to believe that he is not able to get any paid time off. Obviously within the formal employment structure, there's a little bit of allowance for paternity leave and pay, whereas conversely, within the freelance structure, there isn't. This meant we had to share around £500 a month, which didn't even cover half of our mortgage. We're very lucky in the sense that we were both looking after our children, so we had help from each other.

So, I learned quickly that I had to work. I was back doing ads within a month of having my baby. I was able to do little bits here and there, especially when my daughter was younger and slept quite a lot during the day. It wasn't easy, because I found I was always 'on' and I didn't feel like I was truly present with her during the first six months, as I was trying to work around her until I had childcare in place.

For my second child, we had a bit more of a plan. I had three months of pay saved, and by this point we were a limited company, and I was no longer a freelancer. This meant that my husband could take some paternity leave for two weeks. In total, I decided to take three months off, and it was much better the second time around. When I came back, though, there was a cash-flow problem, because I'd almost gone down to zero in my bank account, and even when I started working again, it took a while for people to pay me. It felt like I spent ten months just trying to catch up from the deficit of being on maternity leave. And I must say, it has made me think that I don't know if I can have another child. It's exhausting, and there are other elements that factor into our thinking around having another baby. We went through baby loss in between our two children, and I don't think I can handle the strain of another pregnancy on my body. But there's also the fact that, mentally and financially, it's exhausting.

I do think there needs to be so much change for freelancers; there's just no cover or contingency. It doesn't ever allow you to be a fully present mum; you're always on the edge, and the maternity allowance is never enough to really allow you to relax into it.

Plan ahead as much as you can

It's such an exciting time, but don't forget to plan ahead as much as possible. If you are a founder, you probably want to set aside some time to think about all your day-to-day tasks in running the business. It will help you set foundations for an extremely detailed handover when you eventually go on maternity leave. From this list of tasks, you can then start to train others in your business to master these responsibilities and help things run smoothly while you are off. In the world of freelancing, planning ahead may mean planning how you are going to share the news with your clients, and working out which projects you might be able to bring forward so you can complete them ahead of your maternity leave. I will caveat all of this by saying you may have to flex your plan, and that is totally normal; babies and parenting can be unpredictable, and so you may have some unexpected things to deal with along the way.

Create a succession plan and manage client expectations

Be open with your clients about the plan for your maternity leave. Will there be someone covering some of your responsibilities? Are they able to get in touch with you? How and when can they get it touch, if at all? How long do you plan to be away from the business for? Be as open and transparent as you can with your plans, and help to manage expectations. If it's possible, put a succession plan in place. Is there someone you work with who can step up and cover some of your responsibilities? If so, invest the time in training them up and give them the opportunity to learn from you as much as possible before your leave starts. Clients are such an important stakeholder in your business that you can never underestimate how important it is to communicate with them as clearly as possible.

Set up the correct processes that can be automated or taken over in your absence

No doubt you have a number of processes in place to help your business run smoothly – for example, email sequences to welcome new customers or processes around invoices. I swear by processes in business but also in my personal life. Before going on maternity leave, make note of every process that you have within your business, and areas where your business could benefit from having a process. As you are going through this process audit, make sure you are keeping a record of every single step within your processes so that you can easily share this with people who may be covering for you when you are on leave. Evaluate which processes could be automated. You could start by identifying tasks that are repeated over and over again. This could be recurring invoices, for example; and if so, you could set this up within a cloud-accounting platform to help. Alternatively, it could be ensuring you have a good email sequence for new customer enquiries through a platform like Mailchimp.

Make sure your employees are fully prepared for you to be off

If you have a team, go through every single part of your plan with them in detail. Do it with enough time to spare – probably at the start of your third trimester, so that they have the opportunity to practise some of the tasks they will be responsible for and get feedback from you. This will also give them time to ask a lot of questions while they still have you around. Don't be afraid to go into lots of detail, even if you think they already know it. There will be lots of intricacies that are second nature to you, but not to your team.

Don't be afraid to take the time off that you need

Maternity leave is such a special time, but as a founder or a freelancer, you will probably feel really anxious about stepping away from your business. You might find it really hard to switch off, but stepping away does have its benefits, and it's okay to embrace this season of motherhood that may be slightly detached from your business. The time away can be a chance to slow down that you probably haven't had in some time; it's a chance to reflect on what you have achieved so far, and what you want to achieve in future. Only you can determine what length of time is right to take off. If you have a solid plan in place, I say trust your gut and try not to have any regrets.

Make a note of your tax deadlines, inform your accountant and prepare your tax liabilities in advance

Part of planning ahead is noting down ahead of time any key dates for tax liabilities and reminding your accountant of these before you go on maternity leave. You might even want to send your accountant calendar invites a few weeks before these deadlines so that everything is prepared ahead of time. Set up calendar invites for yourself, too; you will be surprised how some days on maternity leave can merge into one, and you don't want to be caught out and get lumped with fines. If you are struggling with any tax liabilities while on maternity leave, then definitely speak with HMRC and agree a manageable payment plan to help you pay off anything you owe in smaller chunks.

Save for your mat leave

Maternity leave and/or allowance typically isn't a huge sum of money, so you will probably need to put extra money aside to help you fund your time off. Bake these numbers into any business planning that you are doing to help you map out how you can save the additional money. Don't be afraid to set yourself a financial goal at the start of your pregnancy that you want to achieve by your third trimester. Please don't put undue pressure on yourself, but I know some people find it helpful to have a goal so that they feel focused.

Words of wisdom from Georgie Coleridge Cole, editor and founder of Sheerluxe

I have long admired everything that Georgie does. She founded the UK's leading online lifestyle magazine in 2007 at the age twenty-six. In this time, she has had three maternity leaves, and she has a lot of wisdom to share.

Be prepared for the juggle, because from the moment you decide you are ready for parenthood, it is all consuming. I am eleven years into parenting, and it doesn't get any easier. But it's one of the most wonderful things you'll ever do – and one of the, if not the, deepest loves you can feel.

I also think it is one of life's greatest challenges, along with running a business. Entrepreneurs are made of strong stuff and born to spin plates, but be prepared to make sacrifices when it comes to your friendships and your own time. Whatever your career path when you decide you're ready to build a family, there is no stopping you. Remember as humans, we can survive on less sleep than we think; remember you will sleep again, that sleep deprivation never killed anyone, and babies do tend to cry.

Taking a long maternity leave when you run a business – certainly in the early days – can seem like a bit of a luxury. Yet you may well approach maternity leave with a different mindset to someone who is an employee. I think for a lot of people who are employees, they get to a point where it's a bit like Christmas – you're ready to zone out. And yes, there's a bit of that, but you'll be amazed to find that you can send an email while you're having your stitches done after labour.

Babies sleep a lot in the beginning, so there is more time than you might think at the start. I certainly had my longest maternity leave with my first. It should really have been the other way around: as your business becomes more established, you can take more time off. But I took three months off. I worked from home; my office was near my house. That's something I really advise entrepreneurs to think about, because you're going to make life that bit harder if you have a long commute. I live within a ten-minute drive of school and the office, and that means I'm able to structure my business day around parenting. I can (just about) get to cross country in the middle of day, then get back to the office and make it up in the evening.

During my first maternity leave, I held weekly meetings in my house while lying on the sofa. With my subsequent two, I went back quicker, but had set times of the day when I would go to the office and be there in person. It tended to be over lunch-time when my baby was sleeping; my team knew I was there for three hours, and that was when they should catch me, otherwise they would have to wait until tomorrow. And that, for me, was the winning formula. For three months at least. The idea of anything longer just didn't work for me and the demands of my business.

After I had my first child, I had a live-out nanny and we paid by the hour. Despite doing a nanny share three days a week, financially we felt it, and I would down tools and run up the street to get home to take over for five o'clock, just in time for tea. It definitely gets easier financially, but we really felt the additional cost of childcare in those early years.

I have a tip when it comes to juggling work and childcare, and that is to have something I named 'floating hours'. It was so draining being on a call one minute and running up that hill the next, so we introduced floating hours, whereby we had a few extra hours we committed to pay for each week. If I really needed another fifteen minutes at my desk to finish something there and then, or I was stuck in traffic, or I just wanted five minutes to get changed, I could make use of that extra time we were paying for. It took the pressure off, and if we didn't use the hours, we would roll them into babysitting.

I want to add something from the perspective of an employer.

As an employer – and I appreciate that this can vary depending on the industry in which you work – and as someone who has run a business for nearly fifteen years employing mainly women, I now employ a lot of mothers, and they are some of the best people I have in the business. I give them flexibility because I trust that they value their jobs, they value the flexibility, and therefore I know they'll deliver. I know they might need to get to a sports day, but I also know they will make up the time. If you don't flex for them, they will not go on working for you.

In turn, I would really encourage people in the early stages of their journey into parenthood to tell their employer they are expecting a child as early as a possible. On my side of the table, it is challenging when your team go on maternity leave. You feel it: it leaves gaps, it impacts your clients, it affects your own workload, and, of course, it costs money. It's a really hard job to replace good people. So, the earlier you tell your employer about your pregnancy, the more goodwill you tend to get.

I would also really urge prospective parents who might be struggling to conceive or are having to go down the IVF route (which is an immense journey) to be open about their situation, if they can. Personal experience tells me that humans are intrinsically kind, and when things feel like an uphill battle and you need to make another last-minute appointment – even if just for some reassurance that all is well – you will value their support.

> *In a similar vein, I would encourage people who have experienced a miscarriage to share that, not only with their seniors, but, if they feel brave enough, with their colleagues too. They will want to support you. And those of them that are parents will understand and sympathise, and know that parenthood and a career is a constant challenge – but that in the end, when you get there, it will be a rewarding one too.*

Building a side hustle on maternity leave

This is a topic super close to my heart; however, I am incredibly aware it's not for everyone, and I don't necessarily recommend starting anything on maternity leave. I built My Bump Pay while on maternity leave with my first child. While I was on my second maternity leave, I launched the resources section of the business, which was a huge labour of love and took months of writing. It was far from easy with a small baby and a toddler! But I am so proud of what I was able to achieve in those months of focused effort. I was able to grow the community by over 7,000 people and launch a new offering to help women navigate the working motherhood journey.

Sometimes I reflect on the journey of My Bump Pay and think it was something I kind of fell into. But then, if I really think about it, I was probably always going to do something like this. I've always done something 'on the side'. In my school years, it was every sport under the sun. I took my athletics really seriously, with my mum chauffeuring me around to different athletics competitions – Linford Christie was my role model. Then, during law school, I ran a fashion blog with one of my closest friends, which we absolutely loved. We travelled, went to fashion weeks and indulged in something we were madly passionate about. Having a side hustle is probably in my blood, because my parents have different ventures, as did my grandparents and my great grandfather. I've grown up seeing my parents doing their side hustles around their day jobs and eventually going on to build something they are really proud of.

I think becoming a parent makes you look at the world differently; you encounter problems that you have probably never faced before, and sometimes you think, *I can't believe there isn't more to help with that problem.* Some women understandably crave an outlet for something they are deeply passionate about. I fall into both of those camps. In my case, I just couldn't shake the idea that women who have big dreams beyond motherhood deserve to be served better and have access to more relatable information to help make their ambitions a reality.

Embarking on a passion project or a side hustle on maternity leave isn't for the faint-hearted. It takes a lot of time, and in the beginning you will wear a number of hats; you're the marketeer, the head of operations, the CEO, CFO and the mum. All while trying to figure out a number of things about your project or business that you've probably never done before, and, at some point, maintaining a day job. It's not an easy ride! At times, I have been exhausted to the point where I've felt like I had nothing left to give. I've considered packing it all in and choosing a simpler life. However, I will say that I've also found it hugely fulfilling! Watching women flourish has been an incredible experience. If you have something you really want to start, here are my tips.

Tips for starting a side hustle on maternity leave

1. Try to establish a good routine with your kids

Easier said than done, I know! But I do think it is incredibly helpful. It is really hard to work when your little ones are around, and so a good routine will help you enjoy quality time with your kids when they are awake, and you can plan around their typical daily patterns. Nap time is a gift! A gift to be used wisely. Being really honest, this is going to be the time when you are going to get the most work done. You will probably have to be super-duper efficient, depending on your baby's nap routines. I know not everyone is 'team routine' for their little ones, but I am a huge advocate for having a good structure. It helps you plan ahead with the very little time that you do have, and that plan will help you figure out how you can create the time to launch or work on your business. I will be very, very honest: at the start, I had huge trouble trying to get my eldest into any kind of manageable routine, so I called in help from a brilliant sleep consultant, who I always say changed my life! She helped me do what was right for me. So if it is something you are finding difficult, don't be afraid to get help. There are great people you can follow on Instagram who give really helpful advice.

2. Consider building a community

I have loved building a community. It has been one of the best parts of this journey for me. I feel like I have people that I'm really connected with. Which sounds like it can't be true, given the size of the My Bump Pay community, but it really is. I get to hear directly from them the things that they are finding difficult, and as a result I get to tailor my offering to them so that I can truly help and serve them. The benefit of building a community on maternity leave is that it will help you really home in on your niche, understand your potential target audience and get decent feedback. All of which should mean that you waste less time focusing on things that won't resonate with your audience. Let's face it, time is precious, so anything that saves you time is a win.

Communities create closer bonds between your brand and your customers, with those bonds increasing the stickiness of your customers. This can be a secret weapon in a crowded market. Take Peloton, for example, one of my favourite brands with a magnetic community. No one can deny the incredible role the community has played in the brand's impeccable growth.

3. Make sure your idea really is a solution for a need – and that people are willing to pay for it

From time to time, we all have brilliant ideas! What makes a brilliant idea viable is that there is a genuine need for what you are offering. Sometimes the genuine need isn't exactly how you imagined it to be, so it's really important to speak to people who are in your target market. Don't just rely on family and friends; go further and survey people outside of your immediate circle, and probe into what they really need in relation to your idea. I did this through an online survey that initially went to my family and friends, and then I got them to send it on to their family and friends, and so on and so on. It was so incredibly helpful. In hindsight, I should've done this much earlier on in the journey. My Bump Pay actually started out as a completely different idea; it was only when I started to listen to my target audience that I really uncovered their true needs. Once I did, honestly, it felt like something just clicked magically into place and everything began to make a lot more sense. So don't do what I did and leave it for later down the line to find out what people genuinely need. Do it as early as you can – and it's probably worth doing it at regular intervals, so you are always delivering exactly what people want, and you have all the intel you need to help you make really smart business decisions.

4. Join community groups

I quickly learned that I couldn't do this alone, so I made sure to join quite a few community groups of people who were starting and running small businesses. Some of those groups were for parents, which were incredibly helpful. One of those groups in particular was called Doing It For The Kids, which is run by this amazing lady who set up a Facebook group for parents trying to raise a family who are also business owners, freelancers and side-hustlers. I learned so much from these groups, as I got to ask all those questions that you think are stupid but that really aren't stupid. It's through groups like this that I met my web designer and a brilliant lawyer. I made connections with people whom I now consider to be friends. I was also part of WhatsApp groups, and in the same way, I was able to ask all the questions I had. I connected with other founders on what was probably a deeper level. We were able to talk a lot about the reality of running side hustles while being super ambitious in our day jobs and our lives as mums. Honestly, these WhatsApp groups have been a lifeline for me, especially during the really tough times. I remember going through a really tough time where I used to work and it was a particular WhatsApp group that was my sounding board and gave me heaps of support to figure out what to do next. So I'm forever grateful to the support of all the people that I've met in the various community groups during this time. And it's no surprise that I think if you are going on this journey of creating a side hustle, or working on a passion project while also working and raising a family, that you can't do it alone. You need the support of other people who are walking down similar paths, and you will need a support network to help you juggle everything.

5. Make sure the numbers add up

You don't have to make it overly complicated, but I would honestly sit down and really work through the important numbers. Make sure that they make sense, not just in the short term, but also in the long term and also take into the equation how much work is going into making your business idea a reality. It's important to assess all the hard work that you will put into this, especially while on maternity leave, so that you can be sure that your efforts are worth it. It's good practice to make sure that people are willing to pay a fair price for what you are offering. One of the ways I did this was to go to my community and ask them how much they would be willing to pay for a potential solution to some of the problems they were facing. It was so helpful to know if I was in the right ballpark in terms of what I was charging. I also spoke to other people who had similar offerings in different spaces to understand how much they were charging. Something that people don't always factor in is your time. Now, it could be really hard to price your time, because there's not a straightforward conversion into pounds per hour, but I would really encourage you to think about the time that you're going to put into this business passion project, and think about how you can embed the cost of your time into the price of the service you're offering. It's really important that you do that, so that you don't fall into the trap of underselling your service or your product. If you are considering a side hustle on maternity leave, it's very likely that you're doing this all on a tight budget, which is totally understandable. It's also very doable, depending on the business idea.

Don't forget to think about how much you need to spend on marketing. How are you going to get this product or service out there? How are you going to convert people into paying customers? All of this will be part of your marketing strategy, which you may want to put some budget behind to help grow your business. Starting out, it's perfectly reasonable to put very little to no money behind your marketing activities at first, as you can achieve an awful lot for free on social media. But give thought to what money you want to invest in your marketing in the medium to long term. Depending on your sales ambitions, you may find that investing money in the right marketing channels will really help grow your business in the long term.

6. Outsource

Although you may be starting things off on a low budget, it might be worth considering outsourcing some elements of your business now or in the future. For me, using Fiverr, the online marketplace for freelancers, was a lifesaver. It allowed me to find affordable support for elements of My Bump Pay that I don't have the skills to do myself – for example, technical parts of the website. On maternity leave, your time is incredibly limited and you won't be able to do it all, so don't be afraid to outsource the bits that someone else can do much better and quicker than you. Platforms like Fiverr are great, as they typically have a huge range of pricing options. You could even go by word of mouth as a way to get introduced to skilled freelancers who could help. Starting out, you will want to keep costs to the absolute bare minimum, but sometimes trying to do everything yourself will slow you down or cost you more money in the long run. I promise you it doesn't have to cost much; I got a logo created for about £20! Later down the line, you might want to invest in a virtual assistant (VA) who can help with elements of your business, like newsletters, expenses or invoice management. There is a long list of things that you could get the support of a VA to help you with.

I work with an incredible lady called Lucy on an ad hoc basis in really busy periods. She steps right in and helps me get things done. I am always so grateful for her help, especially as my hands are very full.

7. Get focused and let go of perfection

If you are anything like me, you will want whatever you are working on to look and be amazing in every sense of the word. But with a lot on your plate, you are going to have to keep a ruthless focus on the really important things, and let go of the nice-to-haves. I use a project-management tool called Trello to help me manage everything I have to do and prioritise the things that are business-critical. Do your best to make sure the basics are done well, and if you can achieve more, then you are flying high. Over time, you can refine and tweak your offering.

8. Know what the opportunity cost is

In the spirit of keeping it very real, I have to share with you what the cost is of working on a side hustle on maternity leave (and even beyond mat leave). The reality is that it takes up a lot of your precious time. Time that could be spent catching up on sleep, socialising or being with your little one. Maternity leave is a really special time, and it's such a rare occurrence that I would think deeply about whether you really want to give up some of that time to focus on a side hustle or embark on a business. There is an opportunity cost, which is largely your time. There will be moments where it's incredibly intense, and there will be moments where your business has strong systems in place, which takes the pressure off you somewhat. Looking back, I know I turned down time with friends while working on My Bump Pay on maternity leave, and even while writing this book I have really had to reduce my social activities, which has been hard, as I love spending time with my friends. I'm grateful to have such understanding people around me. In a nutshell, there are seasons, but in the early days a lot of things that need to happen will be dependent on you devoting your time. So be prepared to put the effort in to reap the rewards.

9. Feel the fear and do it anyway

The hardest part is getting over this sense that you might fail before you have even begun. So many of us doubt our ability to step out and act on an idea or try something new. Myself included. It took several months of conversations with friends and my husband to even start anything around My Bump Pay. I started by going to Tesco and buying A3 paper, and sketching out what I wanted the website to look like and who I wanted to build this community for. From experience, just starting and learning was one of the best things I ever did. By starting, you will honestly discover so many wonderful things about yourself that you probably never had the chance to explore before. You will learn that you are stronger and more resourceful, agile and creative than you have probably given yourself credit for. To get started, you have to take a leap of faith and believe in yourself; believe that something wonderful will come from this experience.

10. Going back to work with a side hustle

You may have built your side hustle as a way of diversifying your streams of income, which means that going back to work is an inevitable part of your plan. I am a big believer in killing it on all fronts, especially when it comes to your day job: giving it your all and delivering exactly what is expected of you. Anything you do on the side should be kept separate and not interfere with what you are being paid to do at work. At times, some elements of My Bump Pay have taken a back seat as I lean in to work, which often means I work late into the night on my personal projects from time to time to get things done. But I try not to make late nights a habit, in order to avoid burnout. You may find that when going back to work after maternity leave, 100% of your focus is on settling back into work and establishing a good routine, which is perfectly normal.

After you have settled in back at work, you may want to give some thought to outsourcing. Yes, one of my favourite topics. What elements of your business can you get help with, maybe from an intern or virtual assistant to help you carry the load? It could be newsletter writing or social media content.

Having good systems in place will help you push ahead in your side hustle and in your career. Automation is the use of technology to complete processes with minimal human intervention. I've found it to be amazing, and think that it should be taken advantage of where possible. It will help you keep things running in the background of your business, so you can ensure your performance at work is to an exceptionally high standard. A side hustle is definitely not easy, but if it brings you joy then stick at it.

Chapter 6
Childcare

Navigating childcare can feel like trying to find your way through the Wild Wild West, so in this chapter I will work through all the different options that you might want to consider, so you can decide how to find the best childcare option for you and your family. I really do believe that childcare is a critical element for a successful blend. Within the blend, there may be times when you lean on more childcare provisions to help you get through a particular season. Naturally, as your career and life demands evolve, so will your childcare arrangements to help you. In a nutshell, childcare is very much about finding the option that suits you best at a given point in time.

Very early on in my pregnancy, I had a doctor's appointment. I think I must have been around seven weeks pregnant. The doctor asked me if she could give me and my husband some advice, to which we agreed. At that stage, being an eager first-time mum, I was all ears to whatever words of wisdom people wanted to shower me with. I remember so clearly that she looked at us intently and said firmly, 'Get your name on the list for nursery now!' She put the fear of God into us that we might be too late to secure a place for child-care, because where we lived was fiercely competitive for good nurseries. We didn't even consider any other option than nursery for childcare. In many ways, she was right; the nurseries that were really good had waiting lists that were years long.

I was deep in the world of Google searches of nurseries in our local area, and created a shortlist of nurseries to visit. I thought it was wise to wait until we'd had our twelve-week scan, and so off we went, sixteen weeks into the pregnancy, to have a look at nurseries. I actually laugh when I look back at that time, because I thought I had a sizeable bump, but in reality it was barely there! But I went along to these nursery visits with my husband, and so began our childcare journey.

I must say it is quite hard to make such a huge decision for what ultimately is a life that means more to you than you possibly know, and sometimes – as in our case – before you have even met your child. We had no idea what the sex of our baby was or what their personality would be like, or how we would be as parents. We had to make a gut-led decision, as well as trying to give our soon-to-be-child the best that we could reasonably afford. It's a really hard decision to make, so I hope to shed as much light as possible on the different factors to consider to help make that decision much easier for you.

How to decide what type of childcare arrangement to go for

There are a number of different options available to you, and in some ways an easy option would be to just explore what others do in your area, as well as your NCT group, but it's definitely worth pondering which option is genuinely best suited for your lifestyle, finances and career. So, let's explore the important things to consider, as well as the advantages and disadvantages of different childcare options.

Important things to consider when it comes to childcare

Cost

The cost is probably the first thing you will need to consider when thinking about childcare. I would be really honest about your finances and work out, with your household income, how much you can afford to spend on childcare. I don't want to scare anyone, but I do want to be honest: if you opt for a private childcare option, you will probably have to factor in price increases. This was something that came as a horrible surprise to us. It might even be worth asking upfront when the next increase may be coming, so that you can plan for it. Don't forget to factor in the cost of a sibling if that is something that may be on the horizon for you. Work into your future financial and family planning how much it would cost for childcare for another child. You might be able to get a sibling discount from certain providers, but not always, so it is definitely worth asking when evaluating the different options.

The commute

For many of us, the commute changed with the pandemic, and now lots of us are working in a hybrid way, which has been brilliant for reducing the commute time and taking away some of the pressures of the childcare drop-off/getting to work on time dilemma. However please, please, please always take into consideration what your commute will be like into work from the various childcare options that you are considering. I say this even if you are working fully remotely at the moment, or in a hybrid way with some time at the office and some time at home. I have seen people change roles and then no longer have an option to work remotely, or who work for organisations who have had restructures or strategic changes that have changed their approach to hybrid working. You always want to make sure you have a reasonable commute into your office location from wherever your childcare is based. I even encourage people to do a test commute if possible, factoring in all the extra time it takes to get your child ready and to nursery before you head to your location.

Work patterns

A very important factor when thinking about your career is being really honest with yourself about what you want to achieve in the next phase of your life as a working parent. There is a strong chance that if you're reading this book, you have big dreams of what you want achieve, and so it is really worth spending some time thinking about what working towards your goal will require in terms of childcare. It might mean you need a nursery really close to the station to help you accommodate the hours you need to work, or you might need to enlist the help of grandparents if your ambition requires international travel. Thinking of the kind of set-up that you need now and in the future puts you in a strong position to work towards your goals successfully.

Advantages and disadvantages of different childcare options

Private nursery

Advantages of private nursery

Length of the days. Some nurseries offer long hours. Some see this as a disadvantage, but if you have quite a long commute or you have a job that demands you work slightly longer than nine to five, then this can be a blessing. The longer hours may take some pressure off, giving you the time that you need to do your job or get to where you need to be. It also means that you don't have to try and figure out any wrap-around care. In my experience, when we had a nursery that started at 7.30am, it was really helpful, as I still had to drop my other child at another location – all before my workday started.

Different learning styles. Because these nurseries are private, some of them offer different learning styles, such as forest schools, Montessori or language-based learning. Depending on your preference and where you live, you may have access to these various options.

Mess is created elsewhere. I quite like the fact that kids get to explore and do all the messy play they like at nursery, without you having to worry about the mammoth clear-up that comes after or glitter paint on the sofa.

Dependability. Largely, if a member of staff is unwell, the nursery doesn't shut and can still look after your little ones (with the exception, of course, of a COVID-19 outbreak). If, on the other hand, you are relying on one person – for example, a nanny – and they are unwell, it often means you have to scramble around to find alternative arrangements at the last minute, or you may find that you aren't able to work that day, as you have to look after your child. I have found the fact that nursery is pretty much always there to be a huge comfort.

Socialisation. It is lovely for your child to have the ability to get to be around other children. It's great for their confidence and helps to positively build up their independence, too. I think it's only fair to point out that if you don't go down the nursery route, there are still plenty of ways that your child can mix with other children. It's just that in the nursery setting, it's baked in and part of everyday nursery life, so there is less effort required to make it happen.

Disadvantages of private nursery

Not all nurseries are created equal. We have tried a few nurseries, and from the many parents I have spoken to over the years, the quality of the service that you get at private nurseries can vary quite a bit. It took a few tries to find somewhere where we both felt happy with the standard of care and learning. Private nurseries should be following the Early Years Foundation framework, but some apply it with minimal effort, while some go over and above to help aid the child's development and eventually help to get them ready for school. So be prepared to really research private nurseries, and speak to other parents if you can to get their first-hand experience. Local Facebook groups are brilliant for sourcing reviews on local private nurseries.

The cost. I breathe a heavy sigh when I think about the cost of private nurseries. They really are astronomically expensive. I've found the closer you are to a large city, the more expensive they can be. Chapter 2 goes through costs of childcare in general, but you will probably find that private nurseries can be one of the more expensive options, especially as there isn't, in theory, any cap on prices, because they are run privately. You will almost certainly have to pay a deposit of some kind, and maybe even a fee to hold a space on the waiting list, or extra fees for early drop-offs and late pick-ups. Children under three years old are generally more expensive, too, and the cost can become enormous if you have more than one child under the age of three in nursery.

The sickness bugs. For me, the sickness bugs kind of fall into both camps, but they can be a nightmare to deal with, so that's why they appear under the disadvantages. Getting a call from a nursery to say that your child has a fever and you have to pick them up within the hour can completely derail you. Sadly, the nursery setting can mean that your child may pick up all kinds of bugs, especially in the beginning, which can be really difficult to manage if trying to blend work at the same time. I must say, however, that it isn't all bad, as it does help to build their immune system against the common infections that are about anyway.

Childminder

Advantages of a childminder

Family-like setting. I have the loveliest memories of being with a childminder as a young girl. The fact that we were in our childminder's house made us feel like it was an extension of the love and care that we got at home. We were quite lucky that our childminder had two daughters that were a similar age to my sister and I, so we were able to play and hang out together. Just as I have described, a brilliant childminder can feel like an extension of your home, which is lovely if you don't feel that the nursery setting is right for you.

You can still use the government Tax-Free Childcare scheme. This applies for all registered childminders, which is a huge bonus in terms of saving money.

A childminder can be cheaper than nursery. The cost varies greatly based on where you live, and also what that childminder decides to charge. So on the whole, you might find that it is a cheaper option than nursery, but this isn't always the case.

Disadvantages of a childminder

Holiday. Your childminder will need to take time off, and so you'll need to find an alternative arrangement at those times, which isn't always easy to do. So you may find that you're using some of your annual leave to cover for your childminder, which can feel like you rarely have time for your own holiday.

Facilities. Some childminders have very impressive set-ups in their homes, but at times nursery will be able to provide a greater range of facilities, such as a wider range of outdoor activities, toys, books and even food options.

Availability. Because they are typically smaller settings than nurseries, and it's harder to add more childminders in one setting, you tend to find that the really good childminders in your local area are already at capacity. They can only take on more children if a child moves on, as opposed to adding more staff members, which nurseries can sometimes do if they have the physical space to do so.

Nanny

Advantages of using a nanny

Flexibility. Nannies can be wonderful if you need the flexibility – for example, if you work shifts or non-conventional working hours. At times, you can often ask for them to stay a little bit longer or start a bit earlier if you need them, which can be brilliant if you get stuck in an emergency. It's the kind of flexibility that is really hard to achieve with a nursery. It's worth mentioning that they are able to look after your little one if they are unwell, so you don't have to miss important work days because of a temperature or diarrhoea. Nannies are also flexible in the sense that you may be able to find a nanny share arrangement, where you have one nanny looking after more than one child. It's a great option if there is someone close by that you may be able to explore the option of sharing childcare with.

Individual attention. You can train a nanny to look after your little one in a way that works specifically for you. For example, if you have a routine that works well but would be hard to implement in a nursery setting, where there are lots of other children to work around, a nanny can be a brilliant option.

Help with extra tasks. The wonderful thing about having a nanny is that you can get them to help with additional tasks during nap time. That could be sorting out your little one's laundry or batch-cooking their meals, which is a massive source of help and means that you have fewer things to worry about.

Familiar setting. The comforting thing about using a nanny is that your little one stays in a setting that they know and love. This has huge advantages for helping them get used to the change of someone else looking after them. Particularly when it comes to things like their sleep routine, it can be incredibly reassuring for your baby – and for you – that they can sleep in an environment that they know.

Disadvantages of using a nanny

Nanny admin. Hiring a nanny comes with lots of extra admin. Unlike the other options, you are the employer, so that comes with all the additional responsibilities of making sure you have an employment contract, have set up payroll and having a workplace pension set up for your nanny. You can get this outsourced, but it is at additional cost. Another option is to use a nanny agency, who can take care of all these things for you, but be mindful that this can be a really expensive option. Some people prefer to use an agency because the additional admin is taken care of, and they can help with alternative options if your nanny is potentially unwell or you need to find a new one.

Dependability. The downside to hiring a nanny is that when they are sick, which can, of course, happen at short notice, it can be hard to find emergency childcare. If this happens a lot, it can be really disruptive, especially with work.

It can be hard to find a good nanny. It is by no means impossible, but you do have to do lots of research, set up interviews, and then potentially organise a trial for a few hours. Word of mouth is often a really powerful way to get recommendations for a good nanny, but don't just take one person's word for it; get as many references as possible.

Grandparents

Advantages of using grandparents

Cost. If your little one's grandparents are willing and able to help, it is an absolute gift. It is, of course, incredibly cost-effective. You may agree to pay towards activities for your little one, as well as food, nappies, etc. This would still work out much, much cheaper than the other options I have listed above.

Trusted pair of hands. Leaving your little one with grand-parents may give you that extra sense of comfort that your baby is with people you trust. Furthermore, your child will probably settle much quicker with grandparents, and it is lovely to see the bond between your little one and their grandparents flourish.

Flexibility. With family, it is much easier to get flexibility if you're running late or you need them to do more hours in a particular week.

Disadvantages of using grandparents

Tensions. It can be difficult to set clear expectations or boundaries with your parents or in-laws around how you want your child to be cared for. With family, you may even sometimes disagree on other things, as that's what families do from time to time. All of this could impact the care agreement that you have for your little one.

Dependability. I think it's wise to be sensitive to the fact that grandparents still have their own lives, and that may clash with what you need from them in terms of childcare. So you may not always be able to depend on them consistently, which may leave you feeling let down. It is certainly worth having an honest conversation around what their expectations are of the arrangement and establishing some form of routine that still allows them time to do the things they love.

Health. Looking after young children is an intense job and requires more energy as your little ones become more mobile and enter the toddler stage. It may be the case that grandparents find it hard to keep up, despite being in good health. Be mindful of the impact it may be having on their overall wellbeing. Some grandparents may not want to admit to it being hard for them, so it is something that you will have to watch out for.

Questions to ask different childcare providers

I have pulled together a handy list of questions to ask when visiting or evaluating the different childcare options you have. You don't have to ask all of them, as some may be answered for you if you've booked a meeting or a tour, and not all of them will be applicable to you.

1. How much does it cost? Are there any discounts available, such as a sibling discount?
2. Are there a minimum number of days that you have to agree to?
3. How many names are currently on the waiting list, if there is one?
4. What routine do they follow? Is it flexible? Does it suit your child's routine?
5. Are nappies, milk and wipes included in the fees?
6. What day of the month do they take payment? Some providers take payment on odd days of the month, which can be frustrating for planning cashflow. Find out ahead of time if it works for you.
7. Where and how do they put the children to sleep?
8. How much outdoor time do the children have?
9. How do they track and encourage development?
10. What methods of discipline do they use for the slightly older children?
11. Do they have flexibility around pick-up and drop-off? Some childcare providers may allow you to pay a bit extra for a slightly earlier drop-off.

12. What are their COVID policies and other sickness protocols?
13. What facilities do they have for older children? Is this somewhere your little one could potentially stay until they go to school?
14. Are there any points of the year that the nursery is closed completely? Lots totally close between Christmas and New Year, as well as for occasional inset days.
15. Can you change your weekly/daily pattern in the future?
16. Do they allow for children to have breast milk?
17. How do they accommodate allergies?
18. What is staff turnover like?

Important childcare considerations

Have back-up childcare options

It may be that you don't get your first option in terms of childcare; perhaps, for example, your nanny has decided to move away. So always have a second option just in case, as issues with childcare can be incredibly time-consuming and disconcerting if they do arise. Some companies provide emergency childcare, so it is worth asking at your workplace. If not, check out the Bubble babysitting app, which I love and has always come in handy for us.

Planning ahead

If you are anything like me, you may be thinking ten steps ahead to school. It's perfectly normal to think about what lies ahead in terms of your little one's education, because it has such a huge impact on your life, career and even where you live. Some schools have school nurseries that you may want to consider. If it is attached to a state school, it can often be a cheaper option, especially when you factor in any government-free hours. The big caveat is that many of them operate on a school timetable, so you may have to factor in wrap-around care and help during the holidays. Going to a school nursery doesn't mean that you will automatically get a place in the linked primary school, but it does give you a feel for the environment and the staff, and you can even build relationships with other parents who you may be connected to in the long run. Another reason why it is perfectly normal to think about schools is because lots of parents find themselves thinking about moving home to find more space, and if you are planning to move to a longer-term family home, then you should take into account what the schools are like in your area, how the school run will impact your working life, and so on. These are all big questions that you don't have to have the answer for straight away, but are helpful to consider when thinking ahead.

Words of wisdom from Maia Liddell

Maia is an executive TV producer and is a solo mum. She has such a refreshing perspective on childcare and shares her sound words of wisdom for anyone who is trying to navigate the complexities of finding the right childcare set-up that works best for their career and family life.

I definitely still feel like I'm figuring it all out. The best thing for me has been to have a plan A, for sure. But I've learned that you've got to have a plan A, plan B, plan C and plan D, and that can be both in terms of what you think you might want, and other options. You might have in your mind you really want a nanny, but there are other combinations that could work well for you, and a nanny could be your plan B or your plan C. It's just about putting options in place, because you never know when your child might be unwell and nursery won't take them, or you're stuck in the office and nursery is about to close, so you have to make an emergency call to get someone to help you with the pick-up. I'm a solo mum, so for me it's all about making sure that there isn't just one childcare solution and that I've got options and places to turn to. And the other thing which ties into that is not being afraid to ask. We're all so terrified of asking people for support or help; I think we feel embarrassed about it, but actually most people really want to help if they can. Especially if they know that you're in a bit of a tricky situation, they'll do what they can to help, and it makes them feel good.

So, I think I've had to sort of really strip down those barriers and ask for help.

I'm definitely surprised by the childcare I've got now. It's not what I thought I would have, so I think it's good to be aware that there are many different ways to cover the hours that you need to be at work – or sometimes it's about covering the hours to make sure that you have a little bit of you time as a single mum. I thought I would end up with a nanny, but I quite liked my little one going to nursery for the socialisation, so I ended up with half-nanny and half-nursery, until one nanny let me down. I panicked and he ended up doing more days at nursery which has turned out to be much better. He's in nursery four days a week, and one of the staff from nursery brings him home three days a week and gives him a bath, so I get that extra time. So, it's really helpful to think about the different ways that the hours can be made up. I asked myself, what's the thing that's making it difficult for me? It was that I was having to race across London; my job doesn't finish until 6pm, and the nursery also shuts at 6pm. I worked out that what I needed was that extra hour or two of support. I didn't need to spend loads of money on a nanny. So it's also helpful to work out what your crunch points are and try to organise your childcare around that.

Chapter 7
Nailing your return to work

The return to work is such a huge milestone and can often feel overwhelming, packed with nerves, fear, emotion, guilt and anxiety. I always promise to keep it very real with you, so I have to point out that on your journey back to work after a baby, you will probably battle all of these emotions and possibly more. However, that doesn't mean that it has to be an overwhelmingly negative experience or something to dread. In fact, I believe that your return is a brilliant opportunity to reset, refresh and achieve great things. I look back at my returns to work, and, though each one was challenging for different reasons, they brought me greater clarity in terms of what I want as well as greater opportunities. I'm here to walk you through how you can make it a positive experience, one where you feel in control and prepared, and one where you can absolutely push on towards your goals. I will cover how to plan for and have a successful return to work, and we'll also look at flexible working, breastfeeding and your return, working towards your goals after your return, a hybrid return and finding a new role after a baby.

I feel really fortunate to have had two returns. My first was in 2018 and my second was during the pandemic in 2020. They were both quite different, and, to be completely honest with you, my first experience was the most intense, difficult and challenging of the two.

So much had changed in the business I was going back to: there had been a temporary change in leadership, I was asked to take on a new role with huge commercial responsibility, I was largely covering someone else's maternity leave, and I had lots of new peope in my team. The environment was rife with politics, which made it really tricky to navigate. I will never forget one day in particular during my first few weeks back. It was a big reset moment for me. I was frantically rushing through Waterloo station, trying to get to pick-up on time, looking like a hot and sweaty disorganised mess, and miserably failing to hold back the tears. The tears didn't stop, they rolled down my face uncontrollably and soaked my scarf, but I kept running, because that is what we mums do – we keep going, despite how we are feeling at times. At that moment, I couldn't for the life of me understand all the feelings that I had been trying to ignore in order to put on a brave face at home and at work. I felt this pain of wanting to make sure that I could be a good mum, but also feeling like I had tons of ambition inside me – and on top of that I was trying to navigate difficult circumstances at work. On paper, I had returned to more opportunities for sure, but I was figuring out how to achieve the goals I had for myself, while, for the first time ever, navigating being a mum and having a corporate job that I wanted to absolutely nail. In fact, I *was* nailing it; the circumstances I had returned to were pretty brutal, and I was doing a good job, but I just couldn't see it at the time. I had to do a lot of work on myself. It was sometimes uncomfortable sitting with my raw emotions and figuring out how I could continue to push on to build the career and life I wanted for me and my family. In many ways, My Bump Pay became a therapeutic lifeline for me. As I was working on myself and identifying that I could turn these challenging circumstances into something positive, I started taking the My Bump Pay community on the journey with me as I figured out what to do – and what not to do – to have a successful return.

The ingredients for a successful return to work

Confidence

Chapter 8 is going to dig into more detail around confidence, but I wanted to touch on it briefly here because it is an essential part of helping you nail your return to work after maternity leave. It's no surprise mums cite confidence as the biggest issue when returning to work. Your whole life has changed; you've been out of the workplace and things have moved on, and you are trying to establish where you belong and how you fit into the organisation. You might feel that all the success capital that you had built up before you had a baby no longer exists. So it is mission-critical to work on your confidence before, during and after your return. In the next chapter, I'll work through some practical tips to help you do this.

Childcare

By now, hopefully you will have read through my many pleas to sort out your childcare as early as you possibly can. Do not leave it to the last minute! Your little one starting in childcare is just as much about them settling in and getting used to it all as it is about you also getting comfortable and getting used to leaving them with someone else. You will be able to focus at work that much better if you trust, and feel secure, in your childcare option. So try not to leave it to the last minute. This includes any settling-in sessions – try to get those in a few weeks ahead of you actually returning to work. Ideally, avoid dropping your child off in childcare for the first time and starting back at work on the same day, as you just won't be able to focus. Chapter 6 will help you with all the important considerations to factor in so you make the best decision for you.

Focus

It is really easy to feel overwhelmed on your return to work, because all of a sudden, your workload has doubled. Now not only do you have a day job, but you also have a life respon-sibility of raising a child. Focus sounds like an obvious ingredient, but this is about focusing on the important things.

My advice is on a daily basis to focus on the THREE things that move the needle, which I list below. Your priority should be getting those things done – and if you get any more than that done, it's a bonus. The key is to not overwhelm yourself, but just focus on the things that will make a huge difference to your goals or family life. You have to be ruthless and ask yourself every day, what three things can you get done at work that will make the biggest impact? I have found it really useful to list out everything I would like to get done and highlight the three things that are really going to make a difference. I have also found project-management apps like Trello to be incredibly helpful.

1. Organisation

Stepping into the world of working motherhood means that you are going to have to be organised if you really want to have a successful return as well as managing your life as a working mum. You don't have to overdo it, but you do have to try to be a few steps ahead. Here are some of the things that you might find helpful.

Sort everything you need the night before

Packed lunches, clothes for the baby/other children, work clothes for you: quick jobs that take a few minutes at night can somehow seem like a big deal during the morning rush, especially when you also have little ones to get ready who don't always comply.

Plan your new routine and leave extra time for mishaps and tantrums

I totally advise doing a run-through of your day if you work in a hybrid way; both a work-from-home day or a day in the office. When planning your routine, leave enough time for unexpected things to happen, especially as babies/toddlers can be so unpredictable – ten to fifteen minutes should be fine.

Outsource where possible

This won't be new to you, but having the ability to outsource certain tasks will help you devote that time to either your work or your little one. Things you can outsource include cleaning, laundry, food shopping, meal prep and dog-walking. During really busy periods of time, I've found it to be a game-changer to have some things taken off my to-do list. Going back to work for the second time, I used a meal-delivery service for my kids' meals, which sent a selection of fresh and nutritious meals to the house that could be frozen and prepped in minutes when they were needed. It was so helpful to have their food taken care of, and also to know that they were still eating healthy meals. The time that I saved from not having to cook really bought me some extra time to focus on work. Outsourcing is a luxury, so of course do weigh up the financial cost of choosing to get help.

2. Ease back into your return

With strong ambitions, you may feel the urge to start back with a bang. But you totally can – and should – ease yourself back into things. Many people opt for a phased return to work. For both of my returns, I used my annual leave to return four days a week while being paid for five days for around three months. A phased return can have benefits for the employer, too, because it allows the employee to settle back in at a pace that helps them get to grips with all the changes, rather than overwhelming them, which can often have a negative impact on productivity during the return phase.

3. Ask ahead about facilities if you are breastfeeding

You don't want to turn up for your first day in the office and have to figure out where to express. You don't have to stop breastfeeding on your return; it won't hamper your career, and it is your choice when you would like to stop your breast-feeding journey. Your employer should provide you a place to express – and that place shouldn't be the toilets. The toilets are not a hygienic option for breastfeeding mothers.[14] Giving your employer advance notice gives them time to arrange facilities if they don't have them currently, and allows you to get familiar with the set-up so that your time express-ing is efficient and comfortable. Getting this all sorted in advance will help you to focus on your daily deliverables and your goals.

Words of wisdom from Dr Brooke Vandermolen

I spoke to Dr Brooke Vandermolen, also known as the OBGYNMum, about her own return and what advice she would give to other women returning to work. Brooke is a friend of mine, an NHS doctor currently working and training as a registrar in obstetrics and gynaecology, and a mum to two children.

My main advice to anybody who is thinking about the return to work is to think about it and plan early. You can't start too early. I would say the best time to start thinking about your return to work is probably when you've been on maternity leave for three or four months, if you're planning to take nine months or a year. You don't want to think about work in that immediate postpartum period, and you want to give yourself some time to settle into life with your baby and reassess your priorities. But thinking early about your return to work will allow you to speak to your employers and to really plan ahead, because we've got lots of things to consider.

So, first of all, you've got to think about your job and how you see work fitting in with your family life. Do you want to work part-time? What are your goals for your career? And also, think about your family size; are you planning to have another baby at some point? What job does your partner do? Are they around for help with picking up, dropping off, and that sort of thing? And once you can answer those questions in your mind and you've worked out how many days a week you're going to work, and whether your job will allow you to work part-time, you can work out what sort of childcare arrangements you're going to need.

Then you'll need to speak to your employers and try to talk that through. For anyone who works in shifts or in the medical field, like I do, often the shifts are planned out in advance, and expressing your interest early might allow you to select, for example, if there's a day that works best for you to have as your day off.

You also need to think about what's going to happen on your shifts on weekends and nights, especially if you are a single parent; this can be really challenging when you head back to work. Who's going to cover during the night if you're going to work the night shift? Again, having those conversations, preparing early, can really help, and means that you can get your pattern of work set up in a way that's going to work best for you.

In the lead-up to returning to work, I'd really encourage you to use keeping in touch days. All employers should allow you to have some keeping in touch days; they are especially important if you work in healthcare or do shift work, just to get yourself familiar with your field again and with any changes that have been implemented in the time that you've been away. You can use that time to go into work, and to get your baby or your child settled in childcare. KIT days will help you plan your return. You might be breastfeeding, for example, and if you're planning to continue to breastfeed when you're back at work, you can use that time to work out if there are any good facilities for you to be able to express your milk when you're at work. Think about what kind of time you're going to be expressing at work, and where the milk could be kept cold while you're still at work for the rest of the day. Again, it's worth having these kinds of conversations with your employer ahead of time, especially if you're going to need fifteen minutes every few hours to be able to pump.

I have two kids. For my first maternity leave, I took seven months, because I felt that worked best for me. I had planned quite far in advance, and I'd chosen the childcare that I would be having. I had things set up so that I would have a nanny share for two days a week. My daughter went to nursery for one day a week, I was off with her for one day, and I had family doing one day. Quite a complex set-up with different things every day, but it worked well for us financially.

When I went back into shift work, I did feel at first like I had been absent for a long time. I was not used to doing the night shifts, and I'd stopped breastfeeding recently before returning to work, which was quite a hard adjustment. But I really enjoyed the 'me time', and I had the time back to focus on work. The feeling that I was able to improve and continue my career while having a child at home was a really positive experience for me, although I felt much more tired than I could ever have *imagined because I was still being woken up regularly during the night and then going to work. Still, I actually loved my time, both at work and at home.*

My absolute favourite part of being a working parent is coming home in the evening when the kids are already home from nursery, and they see me walk through the door with absolute joy on their faces. They ask me about my day. They want to know what I've been up to, and my favourite hour is that hour when I get home to get them ready for bed. Although I'm tired from my working day, I feel like that hour fills up my cup. I don't resent the kids. I don't need my phone. We just kind of spend quality time together, and that is the highlight for me. So, although there are so many challenges being a working parent, I find work extremely fulfilling. Ultimately, my kids will grow up and I will have a career I can be proud of that I've achieved even while balancing all of that.

Getting ahead after your return – achieving your goals

This section is at the very core of my mission, and is personally very close to my heart. I really want to see every woman who returns to work have the opportunities to achieve everything that they are capable of doing, because I think mums make incredible employees and impactful leaders, and we need more of us holding senior positions in companies to really effect long-lasting change. This part of the book will get into the detail around the key things you need to help you get ahead shortly after your return and beyond. In many ways, this is the stage of the journey where you shouldn't be afraid of the blend; the role of motherhood adds so many valuable strings to your bow and, vice versa; your goals are an important part of who you are. You shouldn't feel that you need to suppress either side of you to be successful. Blend them as beautifully as you see fit.

Sponsorship

First, I want to explore sponsorship, something that cropped up in Chapter 3 and in Deborah Ajaja's story. Without a shadow of doubt, as a female returning to the workplace, you need a sponsor. A brilliant piece of research from Catalyst sums up why perfectly. Their research shows that women are typically behind men in the talent pipeline, even if they have received mentoring. What makes a difference to a woman's trajectory is when they have a mentor who is seated in a position of influence – otherwise known as a sponsor. Sponsors can do more than give career advice; in fact, they are often able to accelerate female talent to the top of the list for new opportunities, and in some instances even remove the list of other candidates.[15]

What is a sponsor?

A sponsor is someone who, in a similar way to a mentor, gives career advice and support. The difference is that a sponsor has the ability to influence important decisions around progression, opportunities and pay. I like to say that they have a seat at the table and the ability to influence at the highest levels within your organisation. I once read that a mentor is someone who teaches you how to dance, and a sponsor is someone who gets you into the ballroom. I think this is a brilliant metaphor, because you still have to master your craft and perform at a high level to have a chance of winning, and the sponsor makes sure the right people know about how brilliant you are. In many instances, a sponsor will advocate on your behalf when those all-important conversations take place about progression at a senior level. I'm often asked if a sponsor can be someone outside of your organisation. Critically, they must be someone within your company, as they need to be aware of your performance and hold those relationships internally to be able to affect change.

How to get a sponsor

It's important to say that finding the right sponsor for you can take some time. It's a relationship that needs to be mutually nurtured. What I mean by that is that it is a two-way relationship. You need to find the right sponsor: someone you trust who can advocate for you in the right way. Simultaneously, your sponsor needs to feel that sticking their reputation on the line will also be of benefit to them. This is the part that people often overlook. Being a sponsor enables someone to prove that they can nurture high-performing talent and contribute to succession planning within a business. A sponsee also becomes a reliable and trusted pair of hands within the organisation, and can also help with initiatives that the sponsor may be working on. Lastly, if they are advocates for diversity and inclusion, they can use their position as a sponsor to have a direct impact on furthering the equality agenda.

There are a few steps you can take to help find a sponsor.

1. Make sure you have a strong track record of exceptional performance and that your achievements are visible – or, at the very least, that you can evidence them easily. Be sure to take opportunities to have exposure to senior leaders where your good work and your strengths are visible. This will make it easier for your potential sponsor to say yes, because they should hopefully be aware of your track record as well as your potential.

2. Map out who you know who has the gravitas and is senior enough to have a seat at the decision-making table. Don't discount someone who has sight of your work, as they are in a strong position to advocate for you as well as advise you.

3. Build the relationship. It would be very odd if you asked someone you barely know or don't have a relationship with to be your sponsor. So it is important to start building a relationship with the person you think

would be a good fit if you don't have a connection with them already.

4. Make the ask. If you have all the above in place, it will increase your chances of getting a yes. Be clear what you want from them, be mindful of their time, and go into the conversation prepared and with the reasons why you want them to be your sponsor. Don't forget to articulate what you are willing to support them with – aka the benefits for them.

Just a quick note about mentors. They too have an important role to play in your journey to achieving your goal after maternity leave. I have found mentors to be pivotal for me, especially in moments where I've faced imposter syndrome or have had professional lows. They have been people who have walked down the path of experience that I'm also looking to walk down. I say all of this because mentoring relationships can be really powerful, especially if your mentor has achieved exactly what you yourself are trying to achieve. Mentors have the added benefit that they can be outside of your organisation, so that can give you more opportunities to find someone who would be an excellent mentor for you. Reciprocity is important here, as it is with sponsorship.

Articulate your goals

Don't internalise your goals when you return to work. It's really easy to do, but equally your return can be the perfect opportunity to vocalise your goals. You will have had some time away from the business, and there will naturally be lots of conversations to catch up on things that have changed in that time. Trust me, these chats are a brilliant chance to share your ambitions. Now is not the time to be shy. You can practise articulating your ambitions beforehand with your friends or your partner.

To help make sure the articulation of your goals has the greatest impact possible, I always say to relate your goals back to the business case. By this, I mean find out what is really important to the business at the moment, and have a think about how your role or skill set can help to have a positive impact on those things. For example, let's say that hiring the best talent is business-critical for your organisation. If you work in the finance department, you could have an impact on hiring by modelling out options to make your organisation more attractive from an incentives and compensation perspective – and that may be important to you, because you want to get involved in more strategic projects that help drive the business forward.

Once you have a good idea of how you want to articulate your goals, share them with your line manager, sponsor and mentor, if you have one. Work through your goals and get to a place where they are agreed with your line manager and sponsor. The next step is to come up with an agreed plan of what you need to do to achieve these goals.

Once your goals and targets have been agreed, you should also make sure early on in your return process that your goals and ambitions have been socialised with key stakeholders, especially your sponsor. Use every appropriate opportunity to remind them of your achievements and any evidence that supports them. Don't forget to collect the evidence of your achievements, ideally in one place, so that they are easy to locate.

Review your return-to-work progress regularly

I suggest a weekly meeting with your line manager and a monthly one with your sponsor. You may feel like this is overkill, but trust me: the return is a huge transition, and these contact points, if used wisely, will help you adapt quickly and make sure that if things aren't working out, you have the ability to review and pivot swiftly. The worst thing you can do is to plough on, struggling through your return in silence. If things are going well on your return, speaking to your manager and sponsor regularly will be a good opportunity to make your achievements since returning known. In these meetings, be sure to find out what you can do to make your boss's job easier, and keep your finger on the pulse. Ask questions like, 'What is important to you now?' 'What do you need to deliver on?'

Words of wisdom from Nishma Robb

Nishma Robb is the senior director of brand and reputation at Google. Mum to teenage twins, Nishma has built an enviable career. She is incredibly vocal about resetting the conversation around diversity, so it was an honour to hear her words of wisdom.

One bit of advice I would give that I didn't do myself (although I wish I had done) is around the pacing of your life. Looking at the way you pace your whole life, including your life outside of work, is really important. As ambitious women, we often want to come back to work in a big way, but that ambition can be unrealistic with the pacing of your life at that particular stage, and it can be really helpful to take a step back and look at all of the milestones across your life. Because what you need at each life stage is completely different. The first five years of your children's lives can be quite intense, and then, as your kids reach school age, the way in which your children need you is completely different. So it is helpful to map out what you need and how you think your life may evolve, then map that back to the type of career you want to build for yourself, the environment you want to work in and the type of company you want to work for. Often, we find ourselves fighting our way through to try and make things work, but we are fighting and making compromises with ourselves. Mapping out your life can bring clarity and help you to design your life and the things you want to achieve in your career. It will help you identify where you need to lean in and what things you may need to let go of.

I never say to women that you have to cut your ambitions because you are a mum; instead, it's about reshaping your ambitions. I think that women who are mothers are incredibly valuable to the workplace; your ability to juggle, manage your time and multitask just becomes better. Before I had children, my time was kind of endless, in a sense, but now I work well to deadlines because I have to manage my time more ruthlessly. Mums are incredible problem-solvers, with a wonderful ability to hack their way through a problem, and they are incredibly persuasive in nature. The skills that you learn as a mother are very transferable to the workplace.

Personally, having kids has given me a real sense of purpose: purpose about what I want to do and what I want for my children, as well as what I should sweat or stress about. Motherhood is incredibly grounding and really helps you work out where you want to get to in life. I once heard a lady talk about working and motherhood as a big social experiment, as we have no idea what kind of impact it is going to have on your child later on in life. I often reflect on that myself when my twins talk about the things I may have missed out on because of work. Actually, I look at their independence and confidence, and their view of women, and I believe that I have done the best thing by them. In many ways, this social experiment is a gift, because the more we talk about our experiences and share them with others and our children, the more they learn – and hopefully their experience of working and parenting will be that bit easier. The same goes for the generation after them.

One thing I can't forget to mention is the financial side of things, which is central to this conversation. I suffered a big hit to my pay coming back to work after having my twins, and it took me five years to get back on par to what I was earning before I had children. I had lost so much of my confidence that I devalued myself, and I felt that I had to compromise on pay because I wanted more flexibility. So, I really want women to know that they can negotiate on other terms, and there are other elements to play with that aren't just pay. It's so important for women to have a sense of their worth and not to devalue their stock, because your talent and capabilities continue to grow while on maternity leave. Financial strength is really important for women as they progress in their careers, especially when you think about things like childcare. I would say that childcare is an investment that pays you back in dividends; you won't regret it later on in your career. It is really hard to see such a large chunk of your pay go towards someone else looking after your child, but it allows you to continue with your career in those early years.

I would also challenge businesses where maternity leave is a reset in terms of a woman's pay or progression. If anything, women should pick up where they left off. Their pay or progression should not be treated as if it is a reset, but more as a continuation of their career and personal development. I would also *encourage women to be really tough on their employer to ensure that parents returning to work don't have to prove their value and their worth all over again.*

Visibility

I often see women tempted to make an under-the-radar return to work. This won't do you any favours. You have been out of view for possibly several months, and so your return is a wonderful chance to show up and take opportunities that allow you to strategically demonstrate your skill set, remind people of your strengths and build relationships.

What is visibility?

Visibility is all about people knowing who you are, your strengths, the value that you add to your organisation and what your contributions have been. It's about showing up at work in a way that allows you to communicate your value through your actions and the right conversations. I see it as the right people knowing why you are valuable, and it doesn't rub anyone up the wrong way. It might also help to think about what visibility is *not*. Visibility is not working hard and keeping your head down.

Why is visibility so important?

Performance and hard work are important, but these factors alone won't get you to your goal. Your hard work, efforts and impact need to be seen. If key people aren't aware of your contributions, then you are more likely to miss out on projects and opportunities that could propel your career to the next level. Visibility is all about staying at the front of people's minds. Other important benefits of visibility are:

- You are more likely to build stronger relationships and become a trusted person within your organisation.
- You are more likely to get the recognition you deserve.
- Your value to the organisation and your team will be evident and harder to question, which helps in terms of opportunities but also negotiations.
- You will feel more engaged in the business, which is helpful when returning to work after maternity leave.
- Senior decision-makers are busy and so they are reliant on prompts or referrals to know which individuals in the business are ready to take on more responsibility for important roles. Being visible helps you to be at the front of their minds for big opportunities that may be on the horizon.

Be intentionally visible

Traditionally, mums have always carried the heavier burden of childcare responsibilities. This means that we are more likely to work flexibly, and we can often miss out on the social aspect of being around colleagues, such as work socials, where meaningful interactions often take place to help promote the visibility of individuals. So, as mums, we have to be incredibly intentional when creating our visibility strategy. What steps can you take to help you increase your visibility? Let's jump into what I like to call the visibility game plan. You don't have to do all these things, but following a few of these steps will definitely help increase your visibility at work.

Visibility game plan: How to stay visible on your return to work after maternity leave

1. Have a clear goal in mind and link your goal to your visibility plan. Ask yourself what you want to be known for and who needs to know about you and your skill set. Lean in to those opportunities that arise and that are linked to your defined goal.

2. In the early meetings with your boss when you return, ask what the key priorities are for the business. You should communicate what your goals are in returning to the business, including asking to be involved in relevant high-profile projects that help further the key business priorities.

3. Spend some time thinking about how your role can make a positive impact on those business priorities. Make a simple plan of how you could be a part of solving those problems, including which initiatives you

---

want to be a part of. You may even spot opportunities to start initiatives to help address some of the key business priorities.

4. Have similar conversations with other key stakeholders to give you a good overview of everything that is important across your organisation. Think about how their responses fit in with the overall aims of the organisation, and how you could help them or incorporate their strategic aims in some of your work. Don't be afraid to bring other key stakeholders on the journey with you. You could get their opinion on relevant projects that you are working on.

5. When you are heading back to work, make sure you are scheduling catch-ups with a variety of people across the organisation, not just your team members. Invest in building genuine relationships. Find out what they are working on, as there could be synergies or opportunities to help each other. Also, ask them for feedback on things you may be working on in your first few weeks. The more people that have a positive experience of interacting with you, the better.

6. Once you have had a chance to soak up all the information and think about where you could have a positive impact, speak to your boss about some of the solutions you have come up with and how you could help.

7. Get a formal or informal plan agreed and follow up with other stakeholders to keep them informed of the plan. Let them know you will keep them updated with your progress.
8. If you have company-wide meetings and there is an opportunity to be present at one of them, don't shy away from being a part of your company updates. For example, you could share client feedback or personal wins that impact the business.
9. Quantify, document and share any wins regularly. Don't be afraid to hype yourself; you will always be your own best advocate.
10. Take other team members on this journey with you and celebrate their contributions and successes too. Help to promote them in front of others.

How to stay visible when working from home

My second return experience was during the COVID-19 pandemic, which forced me to think really hard about how to be visible when working remotely. The pandemic shook up the traditional office set-up, and many of us are now working partly from home and partly from the office.

Don't shy away from video calls

Connecting face to face, even if it is over a screen, is so powerful, especially if you have been on maternity leave. There is a huge benefit to people seeing you if you have been out of the office for a while, as so much of our communication is non-verbal. It would be a huge shame to not utilise all the communication tools available to you. Don't worry about looking perfect or children running in; just show up, give your best and be yourself.

Connect with people from different teams

Working from home, it's easy to connect with just your team and spend very little time connecting with others. Virtual working has removed some barriers, and now it can be easier to set up meetings with people from other teams and departments. So make an effort to schedule time with people from other teams that your work has crossover with. It will help in terms of stretching your ideas or aligning on important matters, and it also helps you to build a wider network across your organisation. Don't underestimate the importance of asking people how they are and connecting on a personal level, too.

Ask for help when you need it

Returning to work remotely can be tricky, and it can be hard to ask quick questions of people as you try to catch up. Asking for genuine help can be a great way to be seen and for others to see that you are teachable and willing to seek advice from those around you with more experience. So, if you are struggling with something on your return to work, don't be afraid to seek advice. Implement the good advice that you get and share your progress with the person who helped you out.

Consider an end-of-the-week or -month update email

Returning remotely may mean that the output of your work is not as easily visible. So you may want to consider sending an end-of-the-week or -month status email summarising what results you have delivered in that time, and what you will be focusing on next. You can explicitly state that the email doesn't need a response, but of course any feedback is welcome. Status emails like this can be really helpful for your line manager, especially if they are across lots of things, and it's also a nice way for you to track your progress during your return.

If you have the option to go into the office and you can make it work – go for it

This may not be possible for everyone, but if you can, go into the office now and again. It could be once every few months or once a week. I highly recommend it. While working from home brings huge benefits in terms of productivity and the logistics of working parenthood, spending time in the office also has its benefits. One of the biggest benefits I have found has been learning from colleagues who are at the top of their game just by being in the same environment as them. Another plus side of spending time in the office is being able to connect and build relationships with a wider array of people. The blend can also benefit from the boundaries that leaving the office can create.

Networking

This word used to freak me out. I'd always thought there's something quite nerve-racking about standing in a room and figuring out how to talk about yourself or trying to discover commonalities with people you have just met. That was until I listened to a podcast where Eva Chen, the Director of Fashion Partnerships at Instagram, was talking about her take on networking, and it really changed my perspective on it all.

Eva talks about how it's really important to keep the door propped open once you have opened it. It's okay to send an email to see how people are doing and stay in touch. It doesn't have to be anything formal, you can keep it casual and just get in touch to wish them happy holidays, for example. You may not get a response, as people are busy, but the important thing is staying in touch, so you don't just save outreach for when you need something. It's not a nice feeling when someone reaches out to you just because they want something from you, nor does it motivate you to help. Ever since hearing this, I have genuinely changed my approach to networking and now it feels more authentic to me and how I like to connect with others.

Continue to invest in your network after maternity leave

This is so important, because the large majority of opportunities come from who we know and not always through a formal process. If you are eager to get ahead after your time away from work, networking can be hugely beneficial. It can help you to find your next opportunity, meet lifelong mentors and increase your visibility. In Chapter 3, I mentioned how much I love LinkedIn as a tool, especially as a working mum, because it's hard to get out and about and meet up with people or attend events on a regular basis. As I've said before, advancement is rarely down to just hard work and luck alone, so continuing to nurture relationships is hugely important.

The approach to networking after maternity leave is very similar to before you went on maternity leave. However, you may find that you have less time than before, so you have to be quite organised with it and weigh up where it will be most beneficial to you. It's so tempting to ignore networking on your return to work because life is incredibly busy, but if you are really keen to get ahead, this is something you can't miss out on.

Flexible working

As a mum, at some point in your career it is very likely that you may need to work flexibly, so it's important to have a handle on what options are available to you, and how to successfully get your flexible arrangement in place in a way that works for you, your family and the business you're working for.

Discussing flexible working should be approached like any negotiation – not in a hostile manner, but in such a way that everyone walks away with some sort of benefit. This means compromise for both parties. I think it's really important to have a flexible mindset when thinking about your request for flexibility, so that the arrangement also works for your company and colleagues.

When requesting flexible working, you want to sell the benefits. Think about your request from the position of your employer; think about their objections, and about how you can positively counteract them.

Tips to help you sell the benefits of flexible working

1. Treat it like a job interview and overprepare before you have the conversation around flexible working. This will help massively with your confidence levels going into the discussion.
2. Have a conversation in the first instance. Avoid submitting your request in writing before having a conversation, because it's really difficult to negotiate in writing. In a conversation, you can get a better sense of the tone and adjust your approach accordingly.
3. Sell your idea. Think through any questions you might be asked beforehand and have compelling points to help overcome any objections.
4. Be ready with solutions explaining to your employer how you believe flexible working might affect the

---

business, and how this could be dealt with. For example, who could cover on the days you're not working?
5. Don't make it all about you. Yes, your desire to work flexibly is inevitably linked to you and your family, but making it all about you will make it tricky for the other party to see the wider benefits of your request.

What are some of the benefits of flexible working for your organisation?

- Research shows that those who work flexibly have a higher level of job satisfaction, and they are more likely to stick around, having put in extra effort into their work.[16] Two in three firms say flexible working helps with motivation, commitment and employee relations.[17]
- It has a positive effect on reducing absence rates.
- It allows organisations to have access to a much wider pool of talent. Flexibility potentially removes geographical barriers and allows parents who may have to work to a slightly different working pattern to still have access to the job market.
- It is an important factor for attracting talent. The best and most attractive companies have a flexible working offering of some kind in order to be able to compete for best-in-class talent. Not to mention it is an important factor for companies who are serious about attracting diverse talent, especially when it comes to careers.

211

- It is the future. An ACAS survey found that half of employers in Great Britain expect an increase in demand for flexible working from employees after the country comes out of the COVID-19 pandemic.[18] In addition to this, there was a government consultation that may see flexible working become a right from the very first day of employment.[19]
- It promotes a workplace culture that empowers staff and trusts them to deliver. The focus shifts to output rather than facetime or man-hours. Empowered staff are more productive and serve clients better, which leads to more profitable businesses.

Your support network

I've mentioned many times just how important a support network is. When I think about women returning to work, I reflect on my own journey and many other women's journeys. A support network is a common thread in people's stories. Not everybody lives close to family, and so how you define your support network is up to you. It could be your paid-for childcare, your friends, neighbours or NCT group, or even your colleagues. These are people who will help you along the way as you blend your family and professional life. Your support network has such an important part to play in your return, and leaning on them often allows you to have greater capacity to push on towards your goals. For me, it's my husband, my parents, my sister, my friends and the wonderful ad hoc nannies that we use from time to time. In fact, there is no way this book could have happened without them. I couldn't do everything that I do without them. I have found that it is so incredibly powerful and helpful to include your support network in your journey back to work. Let them know what your plan is for your return – i.e. what days or hours you will be working, and whether you'll be working from home or from the office. For the first few weeks of your return, it might be a good idea to have them chip in a bit if possible on evenings or weekends while you adjust to your new routine.

Friends are an important part of this journey. There will be good days, when you feel like you are nailing the whole working mum thing, and there will be days when it feels desperately difficult. On those hard days, friends that get it will give you the help and the perspective you need to get through. I'm sure that the reverse will happen, too, and your friends will sometimes need you. I've also found your support network can hold you accountable to the goals that you want to achieve on your return. They will spur you on and encourage you to keep going.

Put in the work

All of the above is important, but you of course won't be able to get ahead without putting in the work. Work smart, work hard, and focus on overperforming around the agreed goals. Refuel when needed, but be prepared to put in the effort.

As you put in the work and have successes along the way, document your achievements. Don't keep your wins to yourself; spread the good news. Make the part that you played clear as you talk about these successes, but do not forget to acknowledge the part that others have played too. Point to how your wins have benefited the business. Hopefully hard work and a strong track record is a given in all of this, but it is important to point out it's the foundation of being able to progress and achieve success.

What if it doesn't all work out as hoped?

I can speak from first-hand experience and say that in our careers, despite enormous amounts of hard work, sometimes things just don't work out as we'd hoped. I have been really disappointed at times in my career before having kids, but in some ways, youth or fewer life responsibilities meant that I could take more of a risk with my career at the time. I'm not saying that you can't take career risks as a working parent, but there are certainly more things to take into consideration. When things don't work out, we should always take some time to reflect on our actions, but also to consider if we are in a positive environment that allows us, as working parents, to succeed. It's a careful blend of the two. While I am a huge believer in taking personal responsibility for our actions and performance, it may just be that perhaps a change is needed, and it might be better to think about the next phase of your career journey.

Finding a new role after maternity leave

There may be a number of reasons why you choose to move on after maternity leave. You may have moved away, feel like you need a new challenge or need a role that is a bit more flexible. As we become mothers, we go through several changes, and I've seen time and time again that it can give women more clarity around what they want to do, or their priorities become more evident, which can ignite change. Yet finding a new role as a mum comes with more complexities and considerations than before having children.

The most important thing is finding a company where you can genuinely thrive as a working parent. So let's break down exactly how you do that.

How to spot a company where you can thrive as a working mum

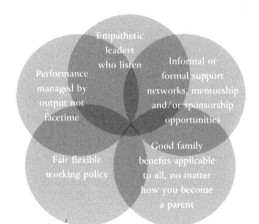

Empathetic leaders who listen

Informal or formal support networks, mentorship and/or sponsorship opportunities

Performance managed by output not facetime

Good family benefits applicable to all, no matter how you become a parent

Fair flexible working policy

This diagram shows the different factors that are important to have in an organisation for a working parent. No company is perfect, so no company will have all these things, but three out of five is a good place to start. I used this matrix to help me scope out what kind of company I wanted to work for after my second child, and it helped me to find an organisation that genuinely had good structures in place to allow me to thrive as a working parent.

Empathetic leaders who listen

These are leaders who take a genuine interest in their people and colleagues. It's not a trait that is essential, but it does help when you are a working mum. There will be things that crop up to do with your children, such as illness, that you will have to navigate, and having a leader who gets it, trusts you to deliver and empowers you to find a solution that works for your career and personal life is really powerful. They don't have to be a parent themselves, but someone who demonstrates empathy for others in their leadership is a positive trait. It's a characteristic that is easily identifiable during the interview stages if you listen closely or even ask about their leadership style. A study by Catalyst showed that when employees feel that their managers are more empathetic, they report being much more able to balance work obligations with family and personal obligations.[20]

Informal or formal support networks, mentorship and/or sponsorship opportunities

This tends to be a feature of larger companies, but plenty of smaller companies offer opportunities to tap into support groups, mentoring and sponsorship. We've talked about the importance of support for mums and mums-to-be at work, and having these initiatives embedded in a work environment is a huge benefit. A company that has these options shows its commitment to allowing working mums to thrive. That is not to say that if they don't, then it's a bad place to be; you could be the person that sets up such an initiative.

Good family benefits applicable to all, no matter how you become a parent

This is an important factor; however, I don't think you should ever join a company for how much they pay for maternity leave. You want to join a company whose policies are inclusive and supportive for women who are mothers and/or may want to become mothers in the future. You should be looking for companies where your career can grow as your life grows, irrespective of how you become a parent. Not all family-related policies are available before the interview, but you can certainly do some research online to see how the company talks about themselves in this area, or how other people talk about their experience as a parent and employee.

Fair flexible working policy

Flexibility for all is important; it is a sign that an organisation is serious about trusting its employees as well as inclusivity and diversity. This has become a non-negotiable for me in my career, and as a parent it allows me to give my very best at work in a way that fits in with my family obligations.

Performance managed by output not facetime

This is an important indicator of an organisation that trusts employees to deliver. Trust leads to better collaboration and better results, and allows people to be themselves. You can also get a sense of how an organisation approaches this at the interview stage. It is hard to thrive in an environment that micromanages, especially when you have to juggle multiple responsibilities at home and at work.

Steps to help you find a new role after maternity leave

1. Before you quit, read your policy

Be sure to have a good understanding of the protocol if you decide to leave your current role. You may have to pay back some of your maternity pay. This may be laid out in your maternity policy, or it may be in your contract or company handbook, so be sure to have a thorough read-through all of the employee policies.

---

2. Get really clear with yourself about what you want and what you enjoy doing

Write it down, really lean in to your strengths, and don't second-guess yourself or hold back as you do this. Use everything that you have written down as your North Star; from there, you can think about what sectors or companies could benefit from your skill set. Maternity leave can bring lots of clarity, so use it to your advantage to find a new role that will be a good fit for you. You owe it to yourself and your little one to be in an environment where you can thrive.

3. Reach out to your network

It's always beneficial to mention to your network that you are on the hunt for a new role. Be as specific as you can with what you are looking for, and ask them to keep you in mind if they hear of any relevant opportunities. You can do this in an organic way, as and when you are catching up with people, or, if you know people in specific fields or organisations that may be of interest to you, then I would let them know early on in your search that you are looking for opportunities. The great thing about your network is that you can also ask what different companies are like in terms of how supportive they are of working parents.

4. Update your LinkedIn profile

This is one of the most powerful ways to get noticed for the roles for which you would like to be considered. You almost have to put yourself in the shoes of the recruiter: if you were a recruiter looking for a particular type of person, what words would you use to search for them? Use those words, and incorporate them where relevant in your profile. Be open-minded when recruiters reach out to you. I say have the conversation, and don't write off too many opportunities at first glance, because you just never know what these conversations could lead to.

5. Sign up to specialist job boards

By specialist job boards, I mean platforms that specialise in roles that are pro-flexible working. This is a growing space and lots of them can be found via a Google search. It is a brilliant way to find roles that are open to some sort of flexibility, which takes away the guessing if you need a job that will be flexible.

6. Practise your introduction

In every interview situation, you will have to introduce yourself, and it is so helpful to have this prepared so that you start off in the most powerful way. This might feel difficult after maternity leave, but if you are struggling, write down your specialism, your strengths, how long you have been operating in this field, and your key achievements. If you can, articulate them using numbers. For example, 'I led the HR division for ten years, and during this time I designed an onboarding process for 150 new joiners, which on average had a feedback score of eight-point-five out of ten.' Pull all these things together and create an opener that is powerful but feels natural to you. Practising it over and over will not only help you *feel* more confident, it will help you *appear* more confident too. Which is just what you need after maternity leave.

7. Stay resilient

Finding a new role can take some time, but do not give up. Use any setbacks and feedback as a gift to set you up for the next phase of your search. I remember so clearly one interview shortly after my maternity leave where I was told, minutes into it, that I wasn't right for the role. Normally I would brush off such feedback and move on, but on this occasion it really caught me off guard – so much so that I remember doing everything I could to keep a brave face and not cry in the interview. I held the tears back, but I was awash with a huge sense of disappointment. But the feedback I was given was truly a gift, and I used it to build on my approach for the next few interviews so that I felt much more ready to take on the next potential opportunities. So the 'no's may sting, but keep your head up; use them to your advantage, take care of yourself, and remember it only takes one 'yes' to change the trajectory of your search.

Chapter 8
Confidence

It's no surprise that mums cite confidence as one of the biggest issues when returning to work. Your whole life has changed; you've been out of the workplace, things have moved on, and you are trying to establish where you belong and how to slot yourself back in. You might feel that all the success capital that you built up before you had a baby no longer exists. There is even research that shows that from six months until two years after having a baby, self-esteem in mothers declines. The good news is that it starts to rise again after year two.[21] A more recent study by Vodafone found that more than a third of all people returning to the workplace after a year or more away experience a drop in confidence, and this figure is twice as high in female returners.[22] In this chapter, I will share with you practical tips to help boost your confidence before heading back to work, as well as things you can do to tackle the horrible mum guilt, and we'll hear from the brilliant Anna Mathur and Sarah Corbett-Winder, two women who give amazing advice on different aspects of confidence.

The Merriam-Webster definition of confidence is 'a feeling or consciousness of one's powers or of reliance on one's circumstances'. After both of my babies, that feeling or consciousness of my own powers was personally a little bit lost. I think the second time around, I was able to rebuild my confidence much faster than after my first child, because I could point to what was happening more clearly and I had the tools to build on my self-esteem.

I haven't hidden how difficult the first six months of motherhood were for me. A big part of this was the feeling of losing myself and, as a consequence, the feeling of losing my identity as an individual, a wife and a professional. Even looking in the mirror was a bizarre experience. A few weeks after giving birth, I hardly recognised my reflection looking back at me because of course my body had been through so many physical changes. All the changes made me question if I still had what it takes to perform at the top of my game. I even questioned whether people would recognise me, and if they would question my ability. I had to do a lot of work on my mindset to really boost my confidence before I headed back to work for the first time.

I know these thoughts aren't unique to me. Granted, not every woman struggles with her confidence after a baby, but it is incredibly common. I guess what I am trying to stress is that if you can relate in any way to what I have shared, you are not alone. This chapter is here to help you find your voice and your power. If you are reading this ahead of embarking on your own motherhood journey, then this chapter is to help proactively equip you with the tools to build your confidence ahead of time.

Why maternity leave may impact your confidence

It makes sense that leaving work for a period of time can really impact one's confidence. Especially when it comes to women who take time out to have a baby. For many of us, there will be someone who steps in to do our role in the form of maternity cover, and the very presence of someone else doing what we used to do can make us question our ability. Organisations can change at such pace that the changes may make you feel as if you no longer know how to navigate the work environment you were used to before. Alongside the changes will probably be new faces, and new people in your team or organisation can make you feel like it is your first day over again. In some instances, you could even be reporting to someone new. Physically, you have gone through a number of changes, and it's perfectly normal for your pre-baby work wardrobe to no longer suit you or fit in the way it used to before. These physical changes can have a deeper impact than just a sartorial one, and all the changes together can take some getting used to. You may even have heard horror stories of people who have been pushed out of roles because of maternity leave. It's so painfully sad when women unfairly lose out on opportunities due to being pregnant or being a mother. But there are plenty of positive experiences out there, so I always encourage women to focus on the opportunities and not on the negative experiences of others, because these can be a detriment to your confidence and self-esteem.

How can you build your confidence before going back to work?

In Chapter 3, I encouraged you to write down your key achievements alongside the key responsibilities of your role before going on maternity leave. If you haven't done this yet, now is your chance. Don't skip this opportunity; find a piece of paper, use your phone, record a voice note or use free space in this book to start scribbling. It is mission-critical. If I could sit down personally with every single one of you to do this, I would. Why is it so important? Because you need to remind yourself exactly what you are capable of. Just because you may not have been in the work environment for some time does not mean that you are not still capable. YOU ARE. It's like riding a bike – you may be a bit rusty, but you haven't completely lost the ability to do it. We do not lose skills during maternity leave; in fact, we gain new ones. One of my favourite exercises to do with women before they head back to work is one I call 'the receipts exercise'. You can use your list of achievements from your day job to help you complete this exercise.

The receipts exercise

Write down three examples that fit into the following categories:

Three career achievements you are proud of:

1. ....
2. ....
3. ....

Three life achievements you are proud of:

1. ....
2. ....
3. ....

The things from your maternity leave you are proud of:

1. ....
2. ....
3. ....

Reminding yourself of your successes past and present is a powerful way of building your confidence. It's not enough to do this exercise once; it's something that you have to remind yourself of often. Alternatively, keep the results of this exercise somewhere visible – on the bathroom mirror, for example. I call it the receipts exercise because, just as we keep track of our receipts as evidence of purchase, we should also keep track of evidence of progress and achievements. I recommend doing this throughout your career from now on – you could even create a little black book of your achievements, or keep a spreadsheet if that is more your vibe. Just make sure to also have something written down in a place where you can see it regularly to give you a frequent boost. If you are struggling to answer any of these questions, then ask for feedback from friends, family and colleagues. People love to be asked to help and hearing their responses is a great way to boost your confidence.

Five ways to build your confidence before going back to work

1. Use your KIT days

KIT days are a powerful tool when it comes to building your confidence for your return to work. I used my very first KIT day to visit a colleague at her house who was about to go on maternity leave. I was due to cover for her during her time off. It was so incredibly helpful to spend the day together to work through big changes, her vision for the work that I was about to take on, important priorities and key projects. I walked away from that KIT day feeling more prepared for my second KIT day in the office. Following the second KIT day, I remember saying to my husband, 'I finally remember what I am good at!' I can't tell you how nice it was to be back to doing something that I knew like the back of my hand vs mother-hood where I felt I was trying to build the plane while flying it! Every KIT day, I grew in confidence in my professional craft. I really can't rave about KIT days enough: when they are planned well in advance, they are really powerful. You can use KIT days for training, too. Some companies offer their returners the opportunity to work with a specialist return coach to help work through their return and work on their confidence. If you are not able to make use of your KIT days, then try to stay connected in some other way; don't go missing on maternity leave. It could just be staying active on LinkedIn or keeping in touch with colleagues. During both maternity leaves, I made a habit of scrolling on LinkedIn while breastfeeding to keep on top of what was happening in my industry and key people moves. It helped me feel so much more confident because I had some touchpoints, and it didn't feel like such a huge learning curve to get up to speed.

2. Invest in yourself

If you are reading this book, then you can tick this box, but it doesn't have to stop there. It's amazing that you have committed to soaking up information to help you nail the working motherhood journey; it shows your commitment to doing the very best that you can and learning along the way. The My Bump Pay masterclasses are an excellent way of bringing all this information to life and helping you to apply it to your day-to-day. You are worth investing in to help you execute the vision that you have for yourself and your family. That investment doesn't always have to be monetary; it could also be time and commitment. Try to set aside time to lean in to free resources, such as podcasts or YouTube videos, to help you find the inspiration and tools that you need. It is 100% worth it; you will learn things about yourself along the way that your nine-to-five can't teach you, and your confidence in what you are able to achieve will soar. I have spoken to women who have completed some professional training or qualification during maternity leave, and while they wouldn't ever want to give the wrong impression and say it was easy to do – in fact, many have said it was one of the hardest things they had ever done – they also said it was incredibly rewarding, boosted their confidence and allowed them to keep taking strides towards their goals.

3. Find your tribe

My tribe is a huge part of my journey. When I doubt myself or I've been nervous about a big next step, it's my tribe that really cheers me on and encourages me to go for it. There is something incredibly special about having a tribe that believes in you, often more than you believe in yourself. So if you are doubting yourself at any point on this journey, don't be afraid to open up to your close friends. They know you well and they know your strengths, and they will remind you exactly what you are good at. Don't neglect nurturing friendships in motherhood. You may feel like you don't have time for others between work and mumming, but I encourage you to cultivate and nourish your friendships. We need a network to hype us up from time to time, and equally, it's powerful to help other women rise.

4. Accept that you won't be perfect as a working mother – and that is more than okay

If you always feel that you need to be at the top of your game, then you will always be second-guessing yourself and doubting your ability. No one person is perfect; we all make mistakes and we are all learning. Swapping stories with other mums can often be one of the most comforting things: you will find that we all have moments and stories that consist of winging it at times. It's totally normal. I find sharing stories and experiences to be a huge relief. Like when I left work on time to pick up the kids, but completely missed my stop and ended up at Gatwick airport, nowhere near my car! I quickly found from sharing my stories that I was in good company, as lots of other mums and dads fessed up to similar experiences. Instead of allowing moments like that to erode my confidence as a mum who is trying to work and look after her kids, I found warmth, encouragement and solidarity.

5. Visualise success

This is a common technique used by world-class athletes. Actually, come to think of it, motherhood and pregnancy can sometimes feel like we are competing in an ultra marathon! So there is no reason not to apply the same technique to help you boost your confidence before heading back to work. Studies have shown that athletes who use visualisation to imagine running a race in their goal time are then able to achieve it. You have to get really specific and go into as much detail as possible. Think about what your first few days back to work would look like: what will you be wearing, where will you be working from, who will you have interactions with, and what will people's perceptions of you be? Visualise yourself confidently walking into the room at the start of meetings; visualise the positive feedback you will get from your first few days back at work. It's a technique I use a lot, especially when I am stepping into unfamiliar territory and I don't want my nervousness to be immediately evident. It has helped me to feel more in control, and has allowed me to focus on positive thoughts rather than negative ones that may never come true.

Dressing for confidence

This is really close to my heart, as I am such a big believer that dressing in a way that makes you feel happy and confident has a huge impact on how you show up. At the heart of it all is a message of placing value on yourself as an individual, and the power that has on you to help you feel at your very best. Don't just take my word for it; there have been lots of studies showing that dressing well has a positive impact on your confidence and how others perceive you.[23] It's a topic that is really worth exploring, because for so many of us, our bodies change after we have a baby. I know how much I agonised over what would fit me heading back into the office, and how much it impacted my confidence. What to wear may be the last thing on your mind, what with everything else that motherhood throws at you, but don't put yourself at the bottom of the pile; there is nothing wrong with spending some time preparing for your return to help you get into the right mindset.

Invest in something new

Invest in one thing that you love. This could be a scarf, a new scent, a new pair of shoes, or even a new haircut. Whatever it is, just make sure you love it. If you love it, you will show up more confident, and this will be clear in everything that you do. Perhaps you can make a day of this shopping trip without your little one. Try to bring along a friend; you won't regret it. It's a great excuse to take some time out for you – and only you – just before you go back to work, especially as you have probably spent months with your little one. This is something I've found to be really important. I appreciate not everyone finds shopping enjoyable, so if that's you, take some time out to do something you love.

The power of a good blazer

A good blazer will never let you down and is a useful piece to own after maternity leave. If, like I was, you are conscious of your tummy area after having a baby, then a blazer is a great way to pull a look together, because it doesn't draw attention to your midsection. Blazers are incredibly versatile and will work perfectly whether you work in a smart environment or somewhere that has a more casual dress code. The wonderful thing is there are good blazers available everywhere, from Primark to Balmain, at every price point. There is something out there for everyone. My most worn blazer is a navy-blue double-breasted number with gold buttons from Marks and Spencer. Honestly, it was the best buy before I went back to work for the first time.

Dress for the role you want

This is something I learned from my dad in my early teens. He was big on us always showing up in a way that was indicative of our ambitions, not just the level that we were already at. It's something that has stayed with me from the day that I started working. I can't say that I've always executed it well, but I've always given it my best shot. It's super important to point out that this doesn't mean dressing formally, because it's not always appropriate to do so, especially if you work in an environment that is more casual or has a uniform. So in these instances, and many others, it is just a case of making sure your hair is tidy, your clothes are steamed or ironed, and that most of all, you feel confident in what you are wearing. An old boss of mine once gave me a bit of lovely feedback that really summed this up for me. He said, 'I always know that if there was ever to be a last-minute client meeting, you would always be ready, because you consistently look the part.' It was that aha moment when I knew that my dad had given me solid advice. We are constantly being evaluated at work, and how we show up is a big part of that. If you show up as if you are ready for your next opportunity, you are sending a powerful message that you are working towards that opportunity.

Get dressed for a hybrid world

Dressing for a hybrid world isn't easy. Lockdown changed the dress code for many of us. For the very first time, we didn't have to worry too much about our full work outfit, and many of us became very well acquainted with elasticated waistbands. I actually went back to work during lockdown, and I really missed getting dressed up for work, as I'd already spent most of my maternity leave in active wear! So even though I was working from home, I used to get dressed to the nines – and if I had really important meetings, I would even wear shoes at my desk. After some time, though, even I (someone who loves fashion) started to get a bit weary of dressing up with nowhere to go, and my approach shifted a bit. It just shows how difficult it can be styling yourself for a hybrid world. I've found that pairing smart tops with comfortable trousers is a brilliant route to go down, because the ensemble will work for virtual calls and also for life in the office. Dressing for the office in many sectors has become more casual. I found that difficult to get my head around at first, because I find it easier to compartmentalise my wardrobe into casual and office – especially as a mum. The casual is typically reserved for activities with the kids, and is therefore difficult to translate into an office environment. In this new era of business-casual fit for a hybrid world, I say don't be afraid of relaxed tailoring: pieces that are tailored but have a bit of a flow. I always think pieces should be balanced, so if you are wearing a boxy shirt, you may want to opt for a slimmer trouser leg, and vice versa: if you are wearing a relaxed trouser, you may want to opt for a more fitted top. This is definitely advisable if you are petite like me.

Brands to try

I've found that certain brands really nail the stylish, timeless classics that make a woman feel chic and put together but not overly done-up, while providing beautiful silhouettes. Basically, clothes that are made well, fit well and aren't too trend-led. My go-to brands in this category are Cos, Marks and Spencer, John Lewis, Massimo Dutti, Arket and & Other Stories. You don't have to restrict yourself to these brands, but if you don't know where to start, the list might be helpful.

Words of wisdom from Sarah Corbett-Winder

Sarah is a mum of three, freelance stylist and personal shopper whose sense of personal style I love. She has a great eye for relaxed tailoring and helps women find their confidence through exploring styles that work best for them. Sarah's words are all about how to dress for confidence when returning to work.

The most important piece of advice I have for someone returning to work after maternity leave is to cut yourself some slack and take the time to be organised, planning what you might wear the night before you go to work. At the same time, I don't know why we are expected to make it into a big thing of having to reinvent ourselves after we have children; I think that we just get wiser.

For me, that means prioritising clean hair, great make-up and eye-catching jewellery. Wear what you feel comfortable in, but try to think in terms of a 'uniform' – this will make getting dressed in the morning much easier.

When I went back to work after having our first child, I was adamant not to be classed as 'a mum now', and I dressed the best I ever have. I was doing a lot of shirts-and-blazer looks with fab gold jewellery. It made me feel great, powerful and ready for any meeting! I have let my style progress and go down a more classic route, but I'll still wear a shirt with one button too many undone, or I'll play with the proportions of a shirt or a trouser leg.

I know this is often easier said than done but if you can have some 'you' time, to meditate, exercise, read or just be, this will make you far more content. A happy 'you' means a happy mother, happy wife, happy friend, and this is at the root of feeling confident. Clothes are then the accessory!

Don't see getting dressed as an obstacle; instead, see it as something that is going to empower your day. I think the main thing is to let yourself feel confident with your clothes. You are amazing; you have just had a baby, which is huge emotionally and physically, and I am telling you that you deserve and should still look fab. And if in doubt, smile.

Mum guilt

We can't talk about confidence as a working mum without talking about mum guilt. It's that feeling that you are not doing enough for your children because of work or other responsibilities. When I ask women in my masterclasses to rank where they are on the mum-guilt scale, with five meaning feeling extreme mum guilt regularly, and one not having any mum guilt, the overwhelming majority score three and above. In fact, I have never seen a one yet. My experiences of mum guilt take me back to the early days of my first return to work. I went back full-time after my phased return was over and, wow, the feelings of guilt were high in those early days. I initially struggled with the idea of working five days a week, because I felt that lots of other parents were working part-time and so were getting quality time with their little ones that wasn't crammed into a jam-packed weekend. As time went by, the feelings of mum guilt decreased as I settled into working full-time. I now experience it in waves, often during intensely busy times when I have limited time to spend with my children. I now know what my trigger is: not being able to carve out a good chunk of time with my little ones where it's just us: no distractions, no emails, and not feeling like I'm being pulled in many different directions.

Mum guilt is hard and I can't deny its existence, as I've personally experienced it, but I also struggle with the term when it comes to working mums. No woman should feel guilty about working to provide for her family, working to reach her goals or working just because she enjoys it. It's more than okay to go out to work and not be with your little ones all the time. Mum guilt also extends to non-working situations when you are out doing something for yourself and not with your children. Time doing the things you love without your children is incredibly important. You should definitely not feel guilty for doing that in any way, shape or form. In fact, I encourage mums to regularly take a break from mumming and get comfortable doing things for yourself. You were you, engaging in the things that you love, for much longer than you have been a mum. I truly believe that creating space for you to indulge in the things that make you happy outside of being a mum makes you an even better mum, partner, friend and employee.

The dreaded mum guilt can be crippling, and it can hold you back from leaning in and grabbing opportunities with both hands, so let's unpack some tips to help you deal with mum guilt.

Tips to deal with mum guilt

1. Process it, accept it, let it happen

I'd heard of this whole concept called mum guilt, but I think I was subconsciously pushing it to the back of my mind, so when it did hit me, wow: it hit me in quite a big way. The second time around, it was much more mum guilt in waves. I know now what it is. I accept it. I process it. I just let it happen. I think the worst thing you can do is ignore it, because it will come back to bite you – and it will bite you hard. It can be quite crippling and can throw you off course. So the first thing I'd say is just allow it to happen, process it and accept it.

2. Don't compare yourself to others

Nobody has it all. Even if they look like they have it all, they don't have it all at one time. So definitely don't compare. Guilt can be evoked by thinking another parent is doing a better job at spending quality time with their kids, or just being a better parent overall. Social media is the worst, because there is no context behind what anyone has achieved or how they are parenting. So don't compare yourself, because you can't compare apples and oranges, and it will do more harm than good. Stay in your lane and enjoy the time you have with your little ones, whatever that looks like.

3. Go through the receipts exercise

You can put a slightly different spin on it this time, and do it in the following way.

Three career achievements you are proud of:

1. ....
2. ....
3. ....

Three achievements as a mum that you are proud of:

1. ....
2. ....
3. ....

Write these things down, and when you are experiencing mum guilt, you can go back to the lists time and time again. Just to help give you an extra boost, say them out loud. Remind yourself that you are doing an incredible job to shape the best future that you possibly can for yourself and your family.

4. Think about the bigger picture

I have printed out Polaroid images of things that inspire me, and I keep them in my workspace. I have images of my family, holidays, Michelle Obama (because she is an absolute boss) and my friends. These images keep me going, and when I'm working and thinking *Oh, my goodness, I should be spending time with my kids instead of working*, they remind me of the bigger picture and why I'm doing what I'm doing. It's been so helpful for me to really visualise it, so I definitely recommend giving it a go.

5. Book a Duracell day

This is a day for you to recharge. The beauty of a Duracell day is that they should be booked in advance on a regular basis. It could be once a month or once a quarter. Everyone around you should know this is your day to relax and recharge. So speak to your partner, parents, sisters, uncles, whoever is going to look after your kids, and make sure you get the Duracell days in the calendar. Happy mum, happy children, happy household.

6. Identify your triggers

Your triggers can take some time to identify, and you might find it easier to write a journal to help you identify the moments you feel mum guilt and what makes you feel that way. I've learned that my triggers are extremely busy times at work. When this happens, I need to carve out some time to spend with my kids that isn't a pressured pre-school pick-up: time where we are doing some-thing that makes my kids – and therefore me – light up. This also applies to spending time with my husband. This time becomes an important factor in how I parent and allows me to head to my day focused and able to bat away the guilt.

Words of wisdom from Anna Mathur

When it comes to the topic of confidence as a mum, there is no one better to speak to than Anna Mathur. Anna is a mum of three, a psychotherapist, author and speaker who is incredibly well known for supporting mums through anxiety, loss of confidence and stress. All of her books are a brilliant resource for mums in the areas of confidence, wellness and anxiety. When I spoke to Anna, she was full of wisdom – and here is what she had to say about confidence.

Lack of confidence can stem from many things, and it can often be a form of imposter syndrome. It is essentially a lack of confidence because you are feeling like you have to act, and there is a bit of you that then fears being caught out or that thinks, Oh my gosh, if you really knew how tired or emotional I am feeling, you would be surprised, or you wouldn't think that I was deserving of the role, or wouldn't think that I was capable. *It's an example of a gap between the 'us' we feel we need to be and the 'us' we are. The bigger that gap, the more our confidence can be dented, because we feel like a fraud. So openness and honesty is really important. Make sure there is someone at work who knows how you're feeling, so that when that little voice says,* If only you knew . . . *well, there is someone in your environment who does know; they support you and they are rooting for you.*

We also need to be really aware of the pressure that we are placing on ourselves, because that lack of confidence is often a result of us expecting too much and thinking that we need to be a certain way. So, how can you start making decisions or just even interacting in a way that feels more authentic? Because that's where confidence is, when we feel like we can be our authentic selves. How can you have some conversations where you just let people in and show some vulnerability? Openness allows you to be more authentic and build your confidence. It's not always appropriate, but how can you ensure that you know there are people around you that you can be authentic with at work?

It's also about nudging your boundaries along in a healthy way, and having the insight to know how to nudge them. Sometimes it's good to say no; sometimes it's good to push yourself and build on that confidence, because growing confidence often happens when we're slightly outside our comfort zone. It's good to check in with your resources and know when it's the right time to nudge your boundaries.

When you're feeling low in confidence, have a written list of things that disprove that. It might be things like 'I was asked back into this job' or 'I was promoted' or some positive feedback that you've received. It is really helpful to have some concrete things in black and white to refer back to in those moments of wobble, which are just so normal.

Chapter 9

Beyond the return – navigating life as a working mum

There isn't much out there to tell you honestly what life as a working mum is like: what to expect and how best to navigate it all to help you achieve your goals. So in this chapter, I want to share with you ways to blend your work and family life to help you stay on track for the success you want. I will talk honestly about the struggles you may face and how to tackle them, and I will share how some amazing women whom I deeply admire manage it, and reflect on their journeys as women with children in the workplace.

It's super important as we dive into this topic that this shouldn't read as if anyone has their life completely sorted. We are all figuring it out as we go, and life constantly throws new parenting and work challenges at us. It's very much like playing dodgeball, trying to figure out how to get to the other side while some balls are coming at us at full speed, some are unexpectedly heading in our direction, and some are flying across the room in what feels like slow motion. As I write this, I feel like I have described my life quite accurately, although sometimes it's like I am playing dodgeball while spinning plates with many of them crashing to the ground. Keeping it very real with you, having children is tough but I say wholeheartedly it is the BEST thing that has happened to me. I have a greater sense of purpose. I have little people whom I love more than anything in this world. I get to pass down the values and the life lessons that my parents instilled in me to my children, which means the special legacy of my parents and their hard work lives on. Everything I do is so much bigger than just doing it for myself; it is for my children. I want nothing more than to see them happy, thriving and growing to be independent, wise and decent human beings who can have a positive impact on our world through their compassion and kindness. On the good days, I pinch myself and honestly can't believe how blessed I feel to be a mum.

On the tough days (of which there are many) I have to dig deep and remind myself of my 'why'. I have to remind myself of my purpose. So I'm going to ask you: what is your purpose? Take some time to answer this question honestly. No one is checking, so don't feel pressured to answer in a way that would make anyone else happy. Think about why you get up to work every single day. Of course, a huge part of that reason is financial, but beyond the money, what are the reasons you go to work? Why do you have the goals that you have? Why are they so important to you? When I dig deeply, some of those reasons, for me, are because I want my children to know that I am working hard to give them the very best that I can.

Another huge factor is my parents. They have worked so hard and sacrificed a lot to give me and my sister the best opportunities they could. I know how much me achieving my goals means to them, and it's a way of saying thank you for everything that they have given me. The very least I can do is show that their sacrifices have not been in vain, and that I am making the most of every single opportunity they have given me. Those are just some of my reasons why, and you may have different or similar reasons. On those days when it is cripplingly hard, don't forget your purpose; it will help to keep you going.

The work–life blend

Ditching the idea of balance has been so liberating for me. Chasing after that elusive work–life balance can be exhausting, and the moment when it clicked that it is more than okay to blend my wider ambitions, family and career was a real turning point for me. It felt like I could stop trying to resolve the fight between the competing demands. Don't get me wrong, there are still points of tension, but I feel like they are all part of the bigger picture, and that family life and work life can co-exist. Also, by embracing the concept of the blend, I feel that we move away from the pursuit of perfection. I find that the pursuit of perfection is dangerous. The image of the perfectly put together woman who breezes through each day, exquisitely prepared for work, never flustered, who arrives in pristine condition just in time for pick-up with a Mary

Poppins-like demeanour, is an absolute myth. It's the pursuit of that myth that leads to mum guilt, imposter syndrome and other confidence challenges. When working with a goal in mind and adding a family into the mix, it can be messy and challenging but hugely rewarding. As you blend your family and work, be sure to celebrate every win along the way. No win is too small; for example, making it through your first day back to work after maternity leave is a win, sorting out dinner after a day in the office is a win, getting some positive feedback at work is a win, and finding time for self-care is a win. All these wins truly make the blend worth it, despite the challenges. The beauty of blending something is that, depending on what you are trying to achieve, you will incorporate different elements in the proportions that you feel are right. Just like baking a cake, a chocolate cake requires a different blend of ingredients to a baked Alaska. Even if you don't know the exact quantities you need, you can keep trying out different combinations until you find what works for you. In many ways that is exactly what life as a working parent is all about: blending and adjusting things as you go! Boundaries are also a healthy part of the blend.

Setting boundaries

Every working mum needs boundaries to survive

Boundaries are super important. I will admit upfront that I am very much on a journey with my boundaries. As my confidence grows in a particular situation, my confidence to implement the right boundaries also grows. Boundaries are healthy; they protect our time and our energy, and they allow us to lean in to the right things at the right time. They are deeply personal. Some boundaries are very black and white and some are more tangible. They apply at work as well as at home. Let's focus on the boundaries that you may want to put in place to help you thrive at work.

Knowing your triggers will help you define your boundaries

I mentioned when talking about mum guilt that knowing what your triggers are can help you keep the mum guilt at bay. Once you have identified those triggers, then create boundaries around them. The triggers don't have to just be in relation to your children. For example, I have to work out regularly. It is one of those things that I love to do and that really helps with my mental health. At the very minimum, I do three high-energy sessions a week. To protect that time, I have put in boundaries in my work calendar to ringfence it a few times a week. Pay attention to the things that make you

251

feel incredibly overwhelmed and use boundaries to help you reduce the intensity of the overwhelm. With virtual working, I have found that my calendar fills up rapidly with meetings. Interactions that can happen so casually in an office environment turn into virtual meetings, which can creep into time that you really have to use to focus on delivering key elements of your role. So protecting your time to make sure that you have clear points in the day is another boundary that can avoid triggering feelings of overwhelm.

Communicate your boundaries

This can be the hard bit. Once you have defined what your boundaries need to be, you will need to share them with key people from time to time, so that everyone has a clear understanding and is on the same page. Don't apologise when communicating your boundaries; sounding apologetic can dilute the impact of your message. My team and my managers know that on a Wednesday, I leave the office early, and they know that during that time, I won't be able to deal with any emails that come in, but I can pick them up once the children are settled in bed.

Defining what counts as urgent is also incredibly helpful. People around you may break those values for things that are urgent, but 'urgent' can mean different things to different people. With your team and your manager, have a chat about what is urgent and where those boundaries can be broken. It's an important part of communicating your boundaries.

If implementing and talking about your boundaries is something you find difficult, I have included a few examples below. Feel free to tweak them to your natural tone.

Scenario: Your boss has the impression you're available 24/7

How you may be feeling:

'I literally don't have a second to do anything on top of what I'm already doing, not to mention trying to balance parenting. It's so clear I'm giving my all right now and struggling to stay sane. I do actually have a life outside of work.'

Here is what you can say:

'I have made a note of what needs to be done and I've ranked it in order of urgency and priority. It would be great to go through this list with you so that we can come to an agreement about what tasks take priority so I can make sure those tasks are completed to the best of my ability. With the amount of work I am doing during my evenings and weekends, I am finding I have very little time to look after myself or spend with my family, so I want to make sure that I can have some time to recharge so I can give my very best at work too.'

Scenario: Impossible deadlines

How you might be feeling:

'There is absolutely no way I can get that done, with everything that I'm juggling at home and at work!'

Here is what you can say:

'I know that this deliverable is incredibly important and I want to make sure I can put my best foot forward and deliver to the best of my ability. I have taken a look and for me to do a thorough job, I will need a bit more time. Can we agree to move the deadline to Monday, and that way we can still meet the client's requirements?'

Scenario: You need to leave at 4.30pm to pick up the kids but you are regularly asked to start new tasks at 4.20pm

How you might be feeling:

'There is no way I can get this done. I want to show I can do a good job, but I have to be on time for pick-up and get to the nursery before they close and give me a fine.'

Here is what you can say:

'Thank you for trusting me with this task. I want to make sure I can get this done within a good time. My hours are

8.30am to 4.30pm on a Tuesday, so if you can get this over to me with more notice next time, I'll definitely be able to get this done and not have to rush it through.'

Delegation can help with protecting your boundaries

So many of us are guilty of thinking that we have to do everything ourselves in order to be seen to be doing a good job, and that means that our boundaries bleed away and become non-existent. If you are a manager or work in a team, don't forget to lean in to the strengths of those around you. You will probably find that delegating tasks that other people are good at means that the task is done to a much higher standard, and overall that reflects positively on the team and frees you up to do your tasks really well. Delegating allows you to supercharge your strengths, which will help in boosting your performance at work.

Tips to keep you sane as a working mum

Staying sane as a working mum isn't negotiable! It's a must! The pandemic revealed that so many working mothers are at breaking point. The world saw the amount of unpaid work that women were doing on top of their day jobs, but this time with no wider support. Unpaid care and domestic work are valued to be between 10 and 39% of the Gross

Domestic Product of the UK, and can contribute more to the economy than the manufacturing, commerce or transportation sectors.[24] I speak to so many women on the brink of burnout because of how much they are taking on inside and outside the home. We have to do what it takes to stay sane, and so I hope these tips will help you.

1. Don't be a martyr

You don't have to do everything for your children. If your child falls sick and you are co-parenting with someone, discuss how you can take it in turns to look after your little one. The burden should not automatically fall on you as the woman; and don't automatically volunteer yourself to take on the burden of childcare without having a conversation with your partner. If you are solo parenting, it can be such a challenge, but speak to your support network and see where they can help.

2. Don't be afraid to outsource

This is definitely a running theme in this book. Outsourcing is so powerful, it really is worth thinking about where it could add the most value and give you the most time back. It can be expensive, but it is an investment in yourself, your career and your wellbeing. My husband and I are really trying to commit to arranging childcare one day a month so that we can have quality time together.

We have both noticed that it has a profound impact on our happiness, our communication and our wellbeing, and overall makes us better parents. During the course of writing this book, I have had to get some help from a nanny, my parents and family for bedtimes now and again so I can make sure I have the time and space to get it done. I've even been known to outsource laundry when it gets out of control. No working mum can do it all, and so from time to time getting help and outsourcing will be the key to staying happy and sane. You can also get creative with it: you could try babysitting swaps with friends and local mums.

3. Make time to live your life and do the things that you love

You have been you much longer than you have been a mum. We wear many hats, but don't forget the most important obligation that you have is to yourself. Don't stop doing the things you love because you are a busy mum who is trying to blend life and work. In her book *The Pie Life*, Samantha Ettus talks about how mums should play in six or seven slices of life. Those slices include children, career, a relationship (or the quest to find one), friends, hobbies, community and health. Samantha says that those women who play in at least six of the seven slices are the happiest. I couldn't agree more! Some of these slices may appear in your life in different proportions at different times, but they are all important. Hobbies are an especially important one, so make sure you spend time on them.

Words of wisdom from Anna Mathur

The incredibly wise Anna Mathur shared some brilliant words of wisdom on this very point.

Where is your place for rest and fun?

Rest and fun are the things that so easily get edged out in pursuit of trying to juggle the things we need to juggle. But rest and fun are actually the things that enable us to function well. So, I really encourage people to have a think about resting intentionally, rather than working towards that state of collapse. We're humans, we're wired to work from a place of rest, we work best from a place of rest. This is really hard when you've got kids and you're juggling everything, but we need to be really intentional about doing those things in our lives that are restful and nurturing. It might not be sleep for you now, it might not be naps. It might just be how are you protecting your nights rather than robbing from your nights to get that space that you're craving? What are you doing that makes you laugh, that makes you happy, that makes you feel like yourself? Often, I think there can very easily be this kind of crisis of identity when people go back to work. I often hear women say, 'But where am I? Where

> am I amidst it all?' You're doing everything, but what's lost?
> What's the cost? Where are you? Where's your fun? Where's
> the sparkle in your eye? Where are the things that make you
> laugh? What did you used to enjoy that perhaps you're not doing
> now because there seems to be no time? How can you try and
> reprioritise those things, even if in a small way?

Progressing in your career as a mum

A common question that comes up a lot is how to negotiate
for a promotion or a pay rise at some point after going on
maternity leave or re-entering the workplace. It's all too common for someone to return to work after having had time
out to raise a child and find they have missed out on a
promotion or pay rise because of it. Now, having come back
to work, they are operating at a level that is some way above
their current role and/or pay, and therefore they want to start
a conversation regarding a promotion and/or pay rise.
However, they often don't know where to start and are scared
about initiating the conversation. I want to break down how
best to approach this, as I think it's an incredibly common
situation that lots of women find themselves in.

Firstly, let's address the mindset. I talked about the maternity
mindset in Chapter 4, and how maternity leave does not mean
that your career is over. I will take any opportunity I can to
repeat this over and over again. You have within you everything it takes to succeed in your career and achieve your goals,

and you have an incredible amount of value, expertise and skills to bring to your role. So the first step is eliminating any limiting beliefs linked to you taking time off for maternity leave.

India Gary Martin, who you will meet in Chapter 11, talks about the 3Ps, which I love. They are a nice way to frame your conversations. The three 3Ps are performance, perception and profile.

Performance. Your performance is a foundational element in many ways, but it is naturally one of the most important elements, as it will be really hard to get paid more than you do now without the performance to back you up. Does your performance really line up with the role that you are aiming for and the money that you feel you deserve? It's helpful to really think that through. Is the ask you are making reasonable based on your achievements? This is why keeping a log of your achievements is really beneficial. It allows you to reflect a little bit more objectively on what you have achieved and ask yourself if it is commensurate with the next level up. If you want to get into the details and really prepare, I would find a job spec for the role you are aiming for, or draft one yourself if there isn't one available. Work through the job spec and align your achievements to the requirements of the role. This is a really powerful exercise after maternity leave, as it allows you to build up a strong and factual picture of where your performance is at irrespective of any time away from work.

Perception. This is all about how others perceive you and how you are perceived within your organisation. Perception is important across the period of time before you go on maternity leave, during maternity leave and after. This is why I actively encourage women to really give some thought to how they want to prepare for their maternity leave, rather than leaving their fate simply to chance. Perception can be actively managed throughout your career, including the time before you go on maternity leave, your return and beyond. It isn't just down to performance; what others think of you at all levels impacts who moves ahead and who doesn't. The political scientist Adam Garfinkle states that: 'Perception matters because only those who are seen in a favourable light by their bosses, peers, and subordinates will continue to move ahead in their careers.' To make sure that you are perceived positively on this working motherhood journey, there are a few key components that you need to have in place.

The first is feedback, which is critical. Not just feedback from people you report to, but feedback from people you interact with at all levels. As you are keeping track of your achievements, keep track of any substantial feedback you get, too. This applies to before, during and after maternity leave. In fact, going off on maternity leave is a great opportunity to ask people for feedback. Be sure to make it something you do regularly and not just at formal performance reviews.

Act on the feedback and rectify any issues. One of my favourite sayings is 'feedback is a gift'. As someone who has been on the receiving end of all kinds of feedback, good and bad, I know the bad can be hard to take on, and it can be particularly hard not to take it personally. But honest feedback can be a game-changer for your career, especially during the working motherhood journey, because your career tends to be linked to important life responsibilities in some ways. So see honest feedback as an opportunity to act and make changes for the better. The feedback, especially in relation to how you are perceived, is super-valuable data that you can use to make improvements that have a positive impact on others, and on your own career, too.

Profile is the final element. This is essentially another way of saying visibility. Do you have enough of a profile in your workplace? Are you visible enough? If you have your head down and you are working hard, but nobody knows about you or the value you bring to the table, it is going to be really hard to push ahead. As a working mum, it is easy to fall into this trap, because we often have to rush off early to get to pick-up on time, which means we keep our heads down and work as efficiently as we can in the hours that we have. Unlike our colleagues without children, we can't keep working non-stop through the evening to get ahead although we may come back online and do some more work later. This forces many of us to be ruthless with our time, or makes us think that we can't attend as many work socials as we would like to. The profile part of this is so important, so it's really worth having a plan around how you can make sure that you have a good profile where you work, and that the right people know about your skills and achievements. You could look for high-impact projects to work on that make a real, tangible difference to your organisation as a way to enhance your profile. Don't ignore the opportunity to build meaningful relationships with key people too. It's a really helpful part of raising your profile.

The 3Ps can't be put into action at the point at which you would like a promotion; the foundations have to be laid over a decent period of time to help you build a positive case around your advancement. It's a huge part of the reason that I really encourage you to use the journey of working motherhood as an opportunity to shape your career where possible. However, I'm very sensitive to the fact that sometimes there are barriers to progression for working mothers that are structural and discriminatory. So in those cases, I know that you can do all the right things and still you may not be given the opportunity to thrive, even though you know you absolutely deserve it.

Having more babies

Part of being a working parent is exploring what the future looks like for your family and your career. This invariably includes whether you want to expand your family. When is the right time to think about adding another child to your family? Similarly to when we explored when would be a good time to start a family, it's wise to take a few key things into consideration.

Are you financially ready for more than one child?

When thinking about your finances, this time you probably have a much clearer picture of how much it costs for your family to bring a little one into this world, what your running costs are currently, and where your costs may change if you were to have another child. One of the biggest costs to take into consideration is childcare, which probably comes as no big surprise. The bite of childcare costs really ramps up with two children, especially if they are both under two years old. Full-time childcare for two children under the age of two costs, on average, £2,100 per month; depending on where you are in the UK, this cost could be slightly less, and in a big city such as London it could be north of £3,000. I think it is so important to be upfront with the costs to take away the nasty surprises that can put a huge amount of financial pressure on people. A number of women wait until their oldest child is close to three years old before they embark on the journey to child number two. This is when significant help from the government kicks in, and families can benefit from fifteen or thirty free hours of childcare and possible tax-free childcare, which makes a significant difference to the bill.

If you have moved companies since baby number one, please make sure you understand and have read your new maternity policy. The same applies to your partner, especially if they have had a change of circumstances. Some companies may state that you have to have returned to work for a particular length of time between babies to be eligible for enhanced maternity pay. In the situation that you go back to work pregnant after your first maternity leave, then as long as you meet the criteria, you will still be eligible for statutory maternity pay.

What are your childcare options?

Aside from the cost, childcare for two little ones is a whole new logistical juggle. You will probably have to examine your current childcare set-up and figure out whether it would work for two children, both from a cost perspective and in terms of logistics. You may not want to keep both children in your current arrangement, or your current set-up may not be able to accommodate two little ones. For example, it may be that the nursery doesn't have space, or if grandparents are helping out, it may be that they can't physically manage two children. Even things like figuring out the commute with two children can impact your decision around childcare. It's a great idea to think about what options you have when it comes to childcare for multiple children, and if you are currently with a private childcare provider, it's worth asking them what their waiting lists are like and if they offer any sibling discounts.

Consider your career milestones

Ask yourself what career milestones are important to you and when you would like to achieve them, taking into consideration any previous maternity leaves and the impact they may have had on your career. It may be that you have missed out on an opportunity you really wanted because you were on maternity leave. Do you know if a similar opportunity may be on the horizon, and do you want to put yourself in a position to fully take advantage of it? You can, of course, still put yourself forward for any opportunity that you want while expecting a child, but if timing is on your side then there is no shame at all in thinking about expanding your family and also mapping out your career goals so they align with your hopes for your family life. Just as Deborah shared with us in Chapter 3, it is totally possible to grow your career and your family at the same time. You have to focus, work hard, be vocal about your ambitions and be visible in your endeavours and achievements.

Ask yourself if you are emotionally ready to have another baby

Lastly, expanding your family is such a beautiful thing, but it really is incredibly demanding on us mothers, and on our partners, too. It is so easy to fall into the trap of thinking that you need to have another baby because of external pressures. But it's important to think about whether you are emotionally ready, and also whether your partner is emotionally ready, as they're an important part of the equation as well. In some instances, pregnancy can be incredibly traumatic, or the idea of going through another birth can spark feelings of trauma. The same goes for postnatal depression. Don't be afraid to work on yourself before embarking on the motherhood journey again. I can highly recommend Anna Mathur and Illy Morrison, who have a range of brilliant services and resources to help in this area. Working on yourself is powerful and is hugely beneficial for your career, too.

I had my two children twenty-six months apart, and it was the hardest thing I ever did. COVID-19 was a huge factor in all of this; learning to be a parent to two little children during a global pandemic was incredibly tough, and there were a lot of tears as I tried to find my strength during a difficult time. I do look back and marvel at how we got through it. A huge part of me just didn't anticipate how much work it was going to be, but now my children are moving away from the baby years, and some things are definitely getting easier. I love the fact that they drive me to keep dreaming big. While the closeness in age was tough at the beginning, I can see that the benefits are now apparent, as they have an incredibly special bond and can entertain each other for a short while. Equally, there are benefits to having a larger gap between children when it comes to your lifestyle and your career. Each maternity leave has taught me so much about myself, given me a clearer vision of what I want to achieve for my family, and brought into focus my own personal goals.

Words of wisdom from Cara O'Leary

When it comes to multiple children and growing one's career, there is no one better to share their words of wisdom than Cara O'Leary, a director at LinkedIn. Cara and I met through LinkedIn, funnily enough, in 2019 when I was searching for mums who were nailing it in their career as a source of personal inspiration. I sent a message out of the blue, and we have kept in touch ever since. She has become someone I deeply respect and admire as she navigates a successful career as a mum of four, doing it all with such humility and gravitas.

*For me, the most important thing is to think about what makes you happy and what you want from your life. Rather than starting at the point of career or starting at the point of family, zoom out – think about further down the line, think about what you **want** from your life. Do you, in the future, see yourself with children, or, when you're older, surrounded by grandchildren? Do you see yourself travelling the world? Do you want to be a CEO? Do you want all of these things? What do you want your future to look like, and how can you make that work?*

Another thing I think about a lot is how not everybody has to do everything at the same time. I often talk about taking turns leaning in at home more or leaning in at work more – but I think we need to take a balanced approach to this. We don't all have to focus on growing our family while gunning for a promotion at work. We need to be kind to ourselves, and to set realistic expectations. We need to think about what works for each of us as individuals, so that we are not putting ourselves under too much pressure, because it can be hard to think, 'I'm going to focus on building my family, **and** I'm going to focus on the next promotion, **and** I'm going to focus on running a marathon, and I'm going to focus on travelling to six different countries.' I would caveat this by saying that I think sometimes women in particular feel that we can't have both. So, we might think, 'Either I can have the family, **or** I can go for a promotion.' At LinkedIn, I see a lot of women who are going on maternity leave, and women who are already on maternity leave being hired in or promoted while on leave.

Even on the LinkedIn platform, I see more of that now – people who call out that they're surprised and delighted to have been hired at six months pregnant, after having shared with the hiring manager that they are pregnant. This is becoming more common in many companies and industries around the world. Common, but not common enough. In a way, it's disappointing that equality in the workplace is seen as a selling point by prospective employees. In another regard, it's still so important that women continue to share stories like these to try and normalise the fact that one could (and should!) be hired at six months pregnant. As employers, we should be hiring people irrespective of their family circumstances, because you should hire the best person for the job.

Arguably, if you hire somebody who's about to go on maternity leave or you promote someone who is about to go on maternity leave, what this can present you with is an opportunity to also hire or promote somebody additional for a period of time to cover this leave. When the first employee comes back from their mat leave, maybe you will have grown as a company, and now you have two opportunities. So by hiring someone else on a contract to backfill the maternity leave, perhaps you have built a great talent pipeline.

As we look at the current hiring market, a lot of companies would be doing well if they had a great talent pipeline that they could tap into right now for the additional roles in their business. And I feel lucky that this is something which, at LinkedIn, we have. Today, 10% of my colleagues are currently on maternity leave (representing 20% of the females in my workplace). This has given us an opportunity to invite other people to step up, taking on stretch assignments and readying themselves for their next play. So I think it's a really beneficial way to look at it from an employer's perspective.

I got some great advice when I was going on my third maternity leave while I was with a previous employer. I had just been to a global sales leaders meeting at our head office, where I met the CEO and all of our Exec Team, and I was really pumped up and excited about my career. I was feeling anxious and concerned about going on maternity leave at such a crucial (I thought) point in my career. In hindsight, I hate that I felt like that. Talk about having my priorities mixed up! But I was at that point in my career where it was exciting, and I really felt like I was going places with this big opportunity ahead of me... but I was due baby number three, so a year of leave was on the cards. The advice that I received at the time was from one of our Global VPs. She was one of the sales leaders, leading our largest account globally. When I shared with her that I felt like this, she told me, 'It's only work. And when you come back, it's all still going to be here. Not that much changes. Everything can change, but not much changes at the same time.' She also remarked: 'Family is more important. So, you need to go and do your thing. When you come back, we'll all still be here.' And she was so, so, so right. It was incredibly reassuring to hear this from somebody else. Someone more senior. Someone who had been there.

As leaders in an organisation, we have a responsibility to share the message for people to understand the part that work plays in our life, but also to highlight that it is just one part. Other parts of our lives can be more important. What work should give us is the ability to live our best lives. It shouldn't and it doesn't need to be our everything, if that's what we choose.

I've learned a lot in the past twenty years of work. I've had four maternity leaves and I have learned valuable lessons each time. I have learned the value of patience, humility and leadership. I have built coaching skills, resilience and tenacity. I have developed as a person, but also as a leader. I understand the need for compassionate leadership. My maternity leaves, and my parenting journey, have been key to my growth and development. I didn't stop learning when I went on maternity leave and then start learning again the day I came back to work; I learned that whole time. Sometimes, I learned more at home than I did at work.

If I were to compare myself with a peer who has been working for the same amount of time without taking four years of maternity leave, I wouldn't feel like I've learned less than them. I would feel like I had opportunities to learn different skills.

I think we need to be very thoughtful about this as leaders, because life experiences and the experiences that we have outside of work can help to shape us, both inside and outside work. I would say, without doubt, the fact that I am a mother has shaped the way that I lead my organisation. There is no doubt in my mind that the fact that I have children and the fact I have to balance means I'm probably more thoughtful about other parents, but also I'm very consciously more thoughtful about people who are not parents who also, of course, have many commitments outside of work.

Something else that has really helped me to think differently and to grow as a leader, which is personal to my journey, is that I've suffered multiple pregnancy losses. I've suffered four losses across two different companies where the approach to fertility or pregnancy loss was quite different. In my personal experience, it has a real impact on employees at companies where it's not *really talked about. Now not only are we grieving, but we are grieving in silence. We don't really have anyone to share that with. We have no support at work, and no one knows what we are going through. It's almost like a secret that we can't talk about, and that makes it inherently more difficult to get past.*

As opposed to in a company where it's talked about openly and we are supported, which is what I had at LinkedIn. Here, it's recognised as a loss and we are given space to grieve. I feel like having the opportunity to speak openly about it and to be met with such compassion – from managers, from peers, from colleagues across the business – this is what makes the difference. It's something that I think people should consider as they think about starting a family, because for some people it happens so easily and for others, it's a long and difficult journey. It's important that we work for a company where our journey to parenthood will truly be supported – irrespective of what path that journey takes.

The last thing that I would say is that, for me at least, having a family helps me to focus my mind. Having important priorities outside of work helps me to think, okay, I've got X amount of time. Like this evening, for example, we have Gaelic football, so when five o'clock comes, I shut the laptop. We need to have everyone out the door by 5.40pm, because to a large degree, my life as a parent is dictated by my sons' schedules, and my desire to be there for them. I firmly believe that there's time to achieve everything. Careers are long.

Personally speaking, if I were weighing it all up again – trying to make decisions around pushing for promotion or starting a family – I would choose starting my family, every time. What I would love, though, is to work in a world where women like me no longer have to make a choice. That's the work environment I want to create for the young women coming after me.

The challenges of being a working mum

No one is superwoman

Speak to any woman who has children and is navigating their career, and they will never tell you that it is easy. It is challenging! The superwoman or Mary Poppins archetype is dangerous and doesn't exist! It needs to be okay for us to talk about those hard moments, listen to each other, empathise and share encouragement. I would hate for any woman to head into working motherhood thinking it is a walk in the park; equally, I don't want to stir up fear, because it is so rewarding – and so very possible – to have a career and be a parent. A big part of the journey is accepting that this idea of superwoman, a woman who has the ability to do it all, is a lie. There are challenges along the way that we have to work our way through and some are harder than others. It should be more than okay, as I hope this book has explored, to discuss our challenges as well as our successes, because that is what makes the journey we are all on more powerful, more relatable and more inspiring to others around us. It also removes the barriers for failure, because when we all realise it's not easy, we can take the pressure off ourselves.

Finding time for yourself

One of the biggest challenges is time. Often, I have felt that I have very little time that belongs to me, which has left me feeling incredibly torn. I have felt the tension between the different people and responsibilities that I need to split my time between. As much as I love to be generous with my time, especially with people whose company I enjoy, I also need time to myself. Solo time is really important to me; it's how I recharge and re-centre myself. It allows me to focus on the road ahead and push on with key actions and tasks. I know lots of you will be able to relate to feeling time-poor.

I'm a big believer, where possible, in claiming time back for yourself on a regular basis. That could be doing an exercise class that you love once a week, going on a solo walk or sitting in a coffee shop alone. As much as we are social creatures, spending time alone can help to strengthen our own mental wellbeing, build resilience, increase happiness and reduce stress. It isn't easy to do when you have little ones and a demanding job, but I am learning to make it a priority – and it is paying off. As mothers, we are leaders in our homes and in our workplaces, so creating the time to look after yourself is important; show up for yourself in small ways every day. You could even do it on your commute to work; or, if you are working from home, can you use some of that time that you would have used to commute to take a fifteen-minute solo walk, for example?

I know some people swear by life hacks to save them time, such as meal prepping, and it does work for lots of people (I've not been able to quite make it work for myself). Other life hacks, such as laying out all the clothes for yourself and the kids the night before, are certainly worth trying. Being intentional and doing a bit of organising can mean that less of your time is swallowed up by running around in a last-minute panic.

Lastly, on time, I want to mention mum guilt again. You shouldn't feel guilty for taking regular time out for yourself. This time is essential if you are to be at your very best at work and at home.

Being treated differently at work

Another very real challenge for many women is how they are treated at work when they are expecting a baby or are a mum. The brilliant campaigner Joeli Brearley from Pregnant Then Screwed says that pregnancy and maternity discrimination affects 77% of working mums. The impact it can have on individuals, their livelihoods and their wellbeing can be hugely detrimental. If you in any way suspect that you are being treated differently at work, I would make a log of what is happening and seek advice from ACAS, a lawyer, Citizens Advice or the Pregnant Then Screwed helpline.

I've encountered situations where some misinformed people have made prejudiced and sexist assumptions based on me being a mother. In that moment, you think, *Did they actually just say that? How can they possibly believe for one second it is okay to say such things?* As much as those individuals weren't supposed to say such things, I did also look at those situations from a different perspective. I've been grateful, in a weird way, that some of those individuals did express their thoughts out loud, as I a) knew what they were thinking, and b) knew that they were not allies in any way, shape or form, and so I knew to manage them at arm's length. I know that it can make you question and doubt yourself in situations where someone treats you differently at work, so I want to assure you that if you are facing such a situation, then the problem lies with the individual being so short-sighted and not with anything you have done. No woman should encounter situations where they are treated differently because of their family circumstances. Discrimination based on a protected characteristic – for example, your gender, or anything to do with maternity, pregnancy, breastfeeding or being a mother – is unlawful. Don't let any superwoman complex make you think any such treatment is okay.

When blending work and family gets tough

There will be points in your work and parenting life when there are competing tensions. After speaking to a number of women, it often seems to happen at the point where you are in a senior role or very much on track to take more meaningful responsibility in your career, and your family life is particularly demanding, typically because your children are preschool age! It is so easy to question if it is all worth it. So many other factors come into play, such as lack of affordable childcare, difficulty with finding truly flexible work, and potentially other caring responsibilities.

I would be lying if I said I have never questioned whether it is all worth it at times. I definitely have! The overwhelm has crept in and made me doubt if I have the capacity to do it all. I'm someone that likes to do everything well at heart, and I hate letting people down. It's that superwoman complex again. The desire or the pressure to do it all, and, in my case, to do it all to an impossibly high standard at all times. Layer that on top of the pressures of a senior role, and I can tell you I have had moments where the collision of work and family has been very real. At times like this, it's been my friends and family that have given me heaps of support and perspective.

Share how you honestly feel with your inner circle – That could be your family, friends or your mentor. Don't fight the tension in silence; talking it through with people you trust

278

will really help. You will quickly discover you are not alone, and that your inner circle will support you every single step of the way.

Drop some balls – It helps to write down all the different things on your plate. What can you let go of? What can wait? There will be something. It could be that you leave the vacuuming for a few extra days to give you some time and space to recalibrate. In some instances, at really busy times, my husband has taken on getting the kids ready in the morning to give me a few more minutes in bed.

Can you make some changes at work? Are you feeling the pressure because you need additional resources for your team? Can you make the business case for an additional hire to help spread the load and therefore make your team more productive and improve results? Can you look at your working day and block out focus time? Uninterrupted time to get through your tasks can really help relieve the pressure of having too much on your plate. Do you need to work more flexibly? If so, then work through Chapter 7 to help you with your request for flexible working.

Words of wisdom from Yewande Ogunkoya

All in all, switching from working and living life without a family to suddenly doing it all with a family is a big adjustment. One that can take time to navigate! I asked Yewande Ogunkoya, a senior leader within the media industry who has worked for one of the largest global communications groups, a mum to two beautiful girls, my best friend and godmother to my son, and one of the smartest women I know, to share her words of wisdom on how she has navigated the adjustment to being a working mum.

'Working mum' – a title that has been bestowed on me for the last five and a half years. Before that, I was just Yewande – never 'Working Yewande', mind you. When was the last time you met someone described as a 'working dad'? I digress. How we see ourselves is so important, because most of us are fighting against what others have decided we should be and what we should feel. I encourage you not to let these titles that are often heavy taint the beautiful and full reality that you are now living. You are a mum; what a privilege. And then you work – whether by choice or necessity, you are managing a career. Neither of these is easy on their own, and combined they're certainly greater than the sum of their parts. These are all things I wanted, independently, but now I must work out how they fit together.

Start by knowing this: nobody – and I mean nobody, I don't care how much help they have – finds this easy. Especially when your children are young. So when it's hard, know you're not weak or lazy or ill-equipped; it's hard because it's meant to be hard. Then know that even if you didn't have children, life's not exactly a walk in the park. This realisation was life-changing for me. What I'd been trying to navigate wasn't simply motherhood and a career, it was control and constraints. Learning how to accept and then enjoy living a life where I can't be fully in control of my time. Where my energy isn't reserved just for me, and where I've got to plan around constraints – especially scheduling and being physically present. 'No, Hun, I can't go to Ibiza next weekend ;-('

Now you understand the lay of the land. It can be a cruel and sudden adjustment to make when you realise your time and energy are no longer yours, but I urge you to first find acceptance and then start to live in this season. Not just survive, but really enjoy it. I'm not going to say smile through the pain. No. If crying in the corner helps, do that – and then get up and get on. The current constraints won't last forever, and I'm told again and again by those who have gone ahead that you'll miss this time when your children are older. So play and spend time with your children as best you can and work as best you can. You can't do both things at 100 per cent all the time, so some days you'll smash work, other days you'll smash mummy stuff, and that is you winning. You are a winner. But don't get conned by that 'doing it all' nonsense. Who even made that up?

And when you're tired, really tired, rest. I'm sure a lot has been said in this book about finding ways to do that, but trust me, you'll love your kids more afterwards.

I started by saying that despite the fact society loves to throw the 'working mum' title around, I am still just Yewande. As

I navigate this busy and full time in my life, I try and make space for things that remind me who I am.

What does this mean for me? Wearing bold lipsticks, blue eyeliner and the highest heels my hips will allow. It's about dressing up to go to work, or to be at home, because dressing up makes me feel good, creative and powerful. It means allowing myself to get lost in unfamiliar streets on a warm day, with no GPS and a curious eye. Crucially, it means if I want to do something, I don't take it off the table. I may have to take the scenic route to get there, as preserving a good state of mental and physical health is so important to me, but I won't take it off the table. Yewande never would.

Chapter 10

For the allies – how can we help working mums and mums-to-be thrive in the workplace?

This chapter will explore why it is so important to help mums achieve success in their careers, and what everyone can do to foster environments where they can thrive. It's an important read for everyone, but specifically anyone who is in management or anyone who generally wants to support mums in the workplace.

For the greater good

Supporting women (including working mums) in the workplace is the right thing to do, and it is also good for business. McKinsey research found that companies with more than 30% female executives were more likely to outperform companies where there were less than 30% female executives.[25] And mums make up a large percentage of the working population of women. So, if we really want an equitable society and equal opportunities for both men and women, we have to advance the careers of women in the workplace, and specifically mothers.

Motherhood is the stage where the differences in pay, work hours and pension holdings really start to become quite stark. A very interesting study[26] looked at reasons for the emergence of gendered gaps caused by motherhood, and overlayed the impact of the pandemic. This study found that the average employment and hours of work of men barely change after they become fathers, while the employment of women falls sharply from above 90% to below 75% after childbirth. For those that stay in paid work, their hours fall from forty to fewer than thirty hours a week. The gender gap in paid working hours stays wide for many years as children grow up. The study goes on to reveal some fascinating figures around how the gap in total earnings grows starkly after childbirth – and what's more, it continues to grow as the children get older. The gap in salaries between men and women exists before parenthood, when women earn about a quarter less than men on average, but within two years of having kids, women's average earnings drop to one half of male earnings, and continue to drop for the next decade. What particularly interests me is that where the women in the family earned the higher wage before kids, they still experienced a similar reduction of hours. This was also evidenced during the pandemic. In families where the woman was the higher earner before the closure of schools, they still had the greater reduction in the number of hours of paid work in order to take on

284

the responsibility of childcare. This is probably due to how we divide domestic and childcare responsibilities, as well as the expectation in society that the work and careers of women rather than men should be deprioritised because of children. If we narrow the gender pay gap, we could add approximately £150 billion to our economy,[27] which further goes to show how important it is to help women to smash the glass ceiling with a baby on the way and beyond. This book definitely isn't about complaining; it's about taking action to improve outcomes. So let's get stuck into what we can do to help accomplish exactly that.

Leave your biases and assumptions at the door

The Fawcett Society found in a study that 40% of those surveyed believed that women were less committed to work once they have a child.[28] This stat doesn't sit comfortably with me. Within the online community that I've nurtured, I have found my experience to largely be the opposite. Many women are simply searching to find a way to make it all work. How can they best navigate the competing tensions with family duties[29] at the same time as pushing on in their career, which they have worked so hard to build? We have to remember that so many of us were working organisations or running businesses long before motherhood. The work of McKinsey and Lean In have actually found that historically, mothers have shown higher levels of ambition than women overall.[30]

Assumptions that label mothers otherwise sadden me and really do stop mums progressing. All mothers should be given fair opportunities, in the same way as anyone else in an organisation. Yes, it may be the case that some working mums adapt how they get things done, but with the right support structures in place, the right person for the job can really flourish. There are plenty of examples in this book alone of women who are forging their own path to success at work and in business who happen to be mothers. These women are not mythical unicorns; there are many like them whose stories are yet to be told, but who are successful in their own right. Therefore, these women serve as brilliant examples that working mothers can be committed to their work, they can operate at the top of their respective fields and they can lead and contribute brilliant results to organisations.

I'm on a mission to change the narrative around working mums not being committed, and to fight against them not being offered opportunities that they can absolutely excel at. So for any aspiring allies, I would encourage you to ensure that working mothers have the opportunity to take on more responsibility and strategic projects. Give them the structure and framework they need to succeed, believe in them, support them, and you will be pleased with the outcomes. Don't let any assumptions or bias prevent you from doing so.

Sponsor a working mum

If you are in a position of leadership where you can impact critical decisions around advancement, consider sponsoring a working mum in your organisation. Support her and her ambition to further her career within your organisation, make sure her contributions and achievements are made clear to those who also hold positions of influence, and mention her name when relevant opportunities are being discussed.[31] The research from Catalyst shows that when women have highly placed advocates, aka sponsors, they rise to the top of the list for opportunities. Use your relationships, network and influence to help further the career of a working mum. Sponsorship is a game-changer for working mums. It is critically important for women who are pregnant, about to go on or return from maternity leave, or working with additional caring responsibilities.

We know from the brilliant research of Mary Ann Sieghart that women are taken less seriously than men.[32] She calls this 'the authority gap', and this gap widens between men and women when you add motherhood into a woman's life. This authority gap is a significant contributing factor to why women do not hold equal senior positions to men in organisations, and why working mums are more limited when it comes to progressing in their career. I have seen first-hand how a sponsor can completely change the trajectory of a mum's career outcomes. As a sponsor, you also have the opportunity to help up-and-coming talent thrive within your organisation, which promotes diversity and talent retention. In addition, by sponsoring someone, you are also building advocates for yourself internally.

Treat returners the same as you would a new starter

For many mums, the return to work is filled with lots of emotions: excitement, nerves and worry. All incredibly similar to how a new employee would feel before starting a new job. There are many similarities between employees starting a new job and returners; a returner could be joining a new team, stepping into a new role, trying to familiarise themselves with new systems and processes, as well as normal changes that have happened over time – so there is lots to contend with. So this period of transition and adjustment needs to be well thought out and planned; it shouldn't be left to the last minute. The first few weeks are an opportunity to re-engage, connect, discuss company and personal ambitions, and get the returner excited about the opportunities ahead.

I've found that this experience has a huge impact on how a returner performs in those first few months, as well as their outlook on the whole working motherhood experience. We've all had experiences of good or bad inductions, and know how much it can impact your first few months in a new company. The same goes for someone who is coming back from maternity leave.

Tips to make someone's return from maternity leave a really positive experience

1. Pull a schedule together of different sessions to help immerse the returner back into work. It could be a combination of meetings and/or reading up on key bits of information. Leave enough time to go through all the major changes within the business and how it impacts their day-to-day role.

2. Set aside some time to talk to the returnee about their ambitions and things they are keen to achieve during their return.

3. Set clear, agreed objectives with reasonable timeframes. Where possible, set the objectives with help from the returner. This will allow them to focus and prioritise their time.

4. Arrange for them to be introduced to new people who may have joined the business while they have been away whom it would be good for them to get to know. It could be as simple as an email to help them build important relationships within the company.

5. Put reminders in your diary to check in with them a few times a month. It doesn't need to be a long meeting but creating time and space to see how they are doing is hugely valuable and will allow you to spot any issues as well as encourage their development.

6. If possible, connect them to someone else in the business who has recently returned from maternity leave. Pair them up as a buddy, to give them someone to chat to who can relate to their experience.

7. Consider investing in your returnees. It could be a My Bump Pay masterclass or a coach. Sessions such as these can help give employees the tools and the confidence to have an impactful return to work. Not to mention, it might engender huge amounts of loyalty and employee satisfaction.

8. Get their feedback. Making the return process as smooth as possible is an ongoing and iterative process. Collecting honest feedback will enable organisations to make meaningful and continuous improvements that actually have a positive impact. Don't be afraid to use the feedback to improve your policies. Policy changes really codify a positive intent to supporting returnees.

A badly managed and poorly thought-out return process is an unpleasant experience and can leave an employee feeling unsupported and unmotivated. A little empathy goes a long way towards creating an experience that an employee will value and in turn be motivated by.

Make it easier for dads to take up parenting responsibilities

To be truly, fully supportive of working mums means also affording a decent amount of support to dads. All too often, the burden of childcare and child-related mental gymnastics falls on the mother; we saw this in its rawest form during the 2020 pandemic. There is a huge opportunity to help working mums avoid the burnout that can happen as a result of bearing too much of the burden on all fronts, and that opportunity is supporting dads when they want to take up parenting responsibilities. Perhaps the best way of putting this into action is by being supportive when dads want to take parental leave. Yet there is still a bit of a stigma attached to dads making use of their paternity leave. They may fear being discriminated against or being held back from opportunities relating to pay or promotion. There may also be a fear of being ridiculed for taking time off. To help combat this, we need more examples of when men taking parental leave has been a positive experience for the employee and the employer. We need these stories to be told widely and boldly to open up the conversation, so that men feel more comfortable talking about the topic and giving it a try. It's so important for allies in this space to champion men who take up parental leave.

In a small study carried out by McKinsey, many of the fathers interviewed said that they felt more motivated after taking leave, and that they were considering staying in their organisation longer. They also said that the leave led them to change the way they work, becoming more productive and prioritising their time better. One dad was quoted as saying: 'Having kids made me very aware of how valuable my time is and where I wanted to place my efforts more strategically.'[33]

The same principle of support also applies to dads who want to embrace flexible working, especially for purposes linked to children. It should be encouraged and supported as a good thing to do. Give dads the right structure and opportunity to make it work and celebrate the success stories so that others feel that they too can give it a try.

Measure, measure, measure

This is for the allies who want to support or challenge the status quo at the next level – or perhaps you're in a position of influence and you can persuade the right people in your organisation to measure the statistics around the progression of working mums. Getting familiar with the data will paint a clear picture of what is happening, specifically if you are able to monitor how working mums are moving through the different levels at work. You will be able to spot trends and start to unpick any successes or identify where more work needs to be done. Measurement is not about measurement for measurement's sake: it's a tool to inspire action in a meaningful way that can be targeted and hopefully bring about positive momentum.

Chapter 11
Finding your way to the top

As this book is about navigating your ambitions while growing your family, I wanted to explore what it is like to operate at the top of your game. I have always been fascinated by the journeys of women who are killing it, and particularly women who are mums and have achieved success. How have they done it? What support systems did they have in place, what risks have they had to take, what have been the opportunity costs along the way? Who has been instrumental on their journey? What challenges have they faced? These are just some of the questions we will explore in these stories, questions I think so many of us are really curious about and want the honest answers to. Success is incredibly personal, and so in this chapter we will hear from four different women who have done incredible things, whom I deeply respect and admire, and who also happen to be mothers. I want their honest stories to inspire you to go for what you want, to build the infrastructure you need to allow you to go for it, and to show that you don't need to let the desire or reality of having a family stop you.

Ambition isn't a dirty word; in fact, I think in so many ways, it's instinctive as you become a mum. You want to provide for your little ones in the best way that you possibly can. I love the way that Karen Brady phrased it in an interview. She said, 'Ambition is that spark inside of you that won't let you settle for anything less than what you think you deserve.' That ambition may fuel and motivate your success; so much so that you really want to be at the top of your game, and you're determined to be while also raising a family. Being at the top of your game is deeply personal and differs for every single one of us. Even as I write this, I'm getting amped up for all the right reasons, because I want every woman who has any ounce of ambition to feel that she has the opportunity to walk the path to her personal success! I'm not ashamed of wanting that for myself and many other women, too.

Words of wisdom from Holly Tucker MBE

I deeply respect Holly Tucker for her role in championing small businesses through her own business Holly & Co, and I personally have benefited hugely from being part of the Holly & Co community group as I built My Bump Pay. Before Holly & Co, Holly founded Notonthehighstreet, Europe's largest small-business marketplace, when her son Harry was a tiny baby. Just incredible really. Holly shares honestly and beautifully such invaluable advice for anyone building something or working hard to achieve a big goal.

I started my first business Notonthehighstreet with a three-month-old baby, Harry. This brought the logistical nightmares you can very well imagine. Yet, what hurt the most, and what stopped me in my tracks as I tried to work or focus on the tasks at hand, was the overwhelming, soul-shattering guilt I felt. I mean, why, when I'd wanted to be a mother for my whole life, was I now handing him over to a nanny and only kissing his head each night as I narrowly caught bedtime? How was my choice to build a business okay? To miss his first steps as he chased a ball in the park? The guilt, and subsequent unhappiness, was overwhelming. Yes, I was rational and understood that I needed to earn money, so I didn't have a choice. I worked to provide for the family and, as he was so small, he'd never really remember this all, anyway! But these wise thoughts could never quieten the whispers of my guilty soul.

I remember my business partner giving me such good advice as I sobbed at my desk at 2am. She said that in a way, building and relentlessly working when he was little would be perfect timing. It would mean that as he grew up, so would the company. When he really needed me emotionally, I would be there to guide him, rather than being at every playdate in the park. And she was right; he is now seventeen, and not only do I have more time, but I'm able to help him navigate his way through the world.

In fact, as Harry grew, our relationship grew. Our 'normal' had been established, which meant he knew I was not doing school drop-offs or pick-ups. He knew Daddy would be at sports day and I wouldn't. He understood what 'quality' time meant and loved the weekend dates I'd create for the two of us – going to the cinema or museums, eating burgers, or even how I helped him feel brave enough to give away his ninth birthday presents and raise money to buy bikes for more disadvantaged children abroad. It made me very aware that the guilt I'd felt before had been wasted energy. It hadn't a) given me golden stars on the 'best mummy' chart that somehow meant my anguish had been noticed or awarded (!), b) guaranteed Harry would 'turn out' better, or c) stopped all the other guilt that consumed my, and most women's, psyche. I still had social guilt ('I haven't called Mum'), self-guilt ('I've not achieved enough today') or professional guilt ('I'm letting colleagues down').

One day, Harry was with me at work aged five because our nanny was unwell. He was under the desk with a DVD player and Wotsits, and he asked me if men could have businesses too. I chuckled and told him 'Of course', and asked, 'Why do you think they can't?' He replied that I was a woman and so he thought only women could run companies! He was very happy to hear that one day, he might be able to have his own business, just like his mum. Believe me, I was a proud feminist that day!

And that is the point. What I say to all parents who share their guilt with me as they build their companies is that we have to understand that what we perceive to be damaging – no-shows at school plays, bake sales or jacket-potato suppers – is actually *the opposite. They are essential lessons that the next generation are lucky to be taught, and their children are the fortunate ones! They have shining examples and first-hand experience of what it takes to be successful; they witness what it means to be an entrepreneur.*

So when I reflect on what my greatest achievements and biggest challenges have been, I think they are wrapped up in one and the same things . . . my wonderful Harry and the incredible businesses I have built in Notonthehighstreet and now Holly & Co, all inextricably linked with the biggest challenges of raising a family and building a business. All one, glorious, messy adventure, the rollercoaster of life, and one that I live in gratitude with, every day, that I am on this planet, doing what I love.

Words of wisdom from India Gary Martin

It is so important that we don't glamourise what it takes to build a career you are proud of and achieve success as a working mum. By no means is it impossible, but it takes a lot of focus, graft, dedication and commitment. One lady that has been very influential on my journey is India Gary Martin. India is perhaps one of the most authentic leaders that I know. Her boldness and confidence to be true to herself has me in awe. India has held regional and global COO and CTO roles for a number of Fortune 500 companies in London, Frankfurt, Tokyo and Hong

Kong. In her final role at JPMorgan in London, India was Managing Director and Global COO for Investment Banking Technology and Operations with multi-billion-dollar management for 15,000 staff in over forty global locations. So it is no surprise that she is a globally recognised leadership expert and sits on the Board of Directors for Euromoney Institutional Investors, PLC.

I would say that it's really important to remember that it really does take a village and that you cannot do it on your own. You cannot have a C-suite job and have kids, and do both well all the time. It's simply not possible. It's not real. The superwoman myth is completely false and it creates this issue where people set very unrealistic expectations; well, not even expectations, but terribly high standards that are not achievable. And so it's that 'it takes a village' phrase that is so widely known that becomes critical to any woman with a family working hard to gain a seat in the C-suite. Making sure you have the infrastructure to support you if you're going to take that kind of job is really important. While I think workspaces and places are moving towards being a little bit more thoughtful about people's personal lives, the reality is most businesses are in place to make money. So they don't care about your childcare issues, and they don't care about the fact that you want to go to your kid's school play. If it works for the business, that's fine. But if it doesn't, their expectation is that you're going to make choices in that kind of leadership role. So if you're going to operate at that level and perform, then you need to have a solid infrastructure in place so that you can manage those two parts of your life.

We have to grant ourselves grace, because it's really hard – really, really hard. And that guilt thing really creeps up, particularly if your job takes a lot of your time, because you can't be in meetings and also be at your kid's school play. You have to make sure that it's a choice that you're prepared to make. You may never be comfortable making it, but understand that sometimes your attention might not be as fully on one thing because it's on another – and that's for either of those things, that's for your family or your job. So, your infrastructure isn't just as it relates to your family; it also relates to hiring wisely the people that support you so that you're not the only one who can do anything, because if you are, you'll fail. You need to make sure that you've developed your staff and your team to be able to take up some of the slack when you need them to, because if it's all about you, and you don't develop people, and nobody else can do what you do, then what happens when you can't? So it's all about infrastructure for me.

My personal experience in the C-suite as a mother was really hard, because most of the women I knew who were in C-suite roles had husbands at home or a partner at home or somebody at home to help with the kids. And my husband worked as much as I did. That didn't give us a lot of flexibility, and so it was really difficult. I had to buy infrastructure. I had to have a full-time live-in nanny-housekeeper. She did a lot for us, she was a *full-time live-in everything. Basically, I had to hire the wife that I would've been had I been at home. So I needed to hire myself, and that's what I call it, because the reality is that women are the ones who carry a lot of that burden in families. But again, a lot of the women that I knew who were in the C-suite had husbands who were either super flexible, or in roles where they could be at home all the time, or they were stay-at-home fathers. If not, they bought infrastructure like I did. And at a certain point, you have to understand that's a part of your bottom-line cost: paying for somebody to help you do all the things that you can't.*

As your children grow, you may find that your career is growing to new heights and the demands on your time increase. My advice to anyone in that scenario is that everybody I know has had a crisis around that. It's the tension between their kids and work. When you can put in time and be present, be present, because especially as your children grow older, they will remember that. My mum worked a lot when I was growing up, but I don't remember there being a gap in her presence. What I remember is that she was always there for the important things, and that is honestly what matters the most.

Words of wisdom from Laura Fenton

You know when you meet someone and you are instantly in awe of their energy? That is exactly how I felt when

I met Laura early in 2021. There was a spark and an ambition that I was immediately drawn to and knew was rare! Then, as soon as I realised that she had children, my respect ratings went through the roof. It is not often that you meet a CEO who leads with such authenticity, warmth and gravitas. As the CEO of one of the UK's leading media agency OMD UK, Laura Fenton is all those things. Her ambition is nothing short of inspiring: she started as a graduate at OMD and she is now leading the charge.

It's a combination of drive and support that have helped me navigate my way to the top with a family. I've always been very ambitious and have refused to believe that I can't be a great mum and also get to the top in my career. I push myself to raise my hand for new opportunities even if they make me feel uncomfortable – I'm a big believer in the saying 'If you throw your hat over the wall, then you have to go and get it!'

I haven't tried to just repeat the way things have always been done, but instead try to find new ways to show up in a leadership role that allow me to create space for work and family, whether that's adopting different flexible working patterns or changing the way we do corporate entertainment in our agency to be more family-friendly.

I also have an amazing support structure. I have a very equal partnership with my husband where everything is shared, from school admin to DIY. I also have a great boss who is a huge ally for women in leadership, and lots of childcare help. It takes a village!!

What words of wisdom would you give to ambitious women who are trying to find their way to the top in their career and navigate family life?

Work smarter, not harder. You don't have all the hours in the day any more to focus exclusively on your job. So plan your time with precision. Think about the three most important things that you need to get done each day, and get them out of the way first. Know when in the day you are most productive, and try and plan your childcare to protect those hours. Say no to things that aren't going to get you to where you need to go!!

Set your boundaries. This is a big one. When you are working in any kind of flexible pattern, as lots of working mums are, you have to set clear boundaries. As much as possible, be focused on your kids when you are with them, and on your work when you are in that mode. Leave your phone downstairs at bath time and zip your laptop into a bag once you have logged off for the evening, as you also need to create time for yourself!

Back yourself and don't be apologetic about your childcare responsibilities. Women, and especially working mums, underestimate their value and feel that they have to compensate for the time they take to be with their kids. Don't! Believe in yourself and the value you add. And find an employer that thinks the same!

Nothing is set in stone. What was working for you last month, might not next month. Kids' requirements change quickly, whether that's the move from nursery to school, or just additional needs they have from time to time. Keep reviewing your working pattern, your support structure, how you balance things with your partner, and where in all of that you find time for you. I call regular 'meetings' with my husband to check our balance, who is doing what, where we need extra help and how things could improve.

Words of wisdom from Michelle Kennedy

In 2014, when Michelle Kennedy was expecting her first child, Finlay, she realised that mums really needed a new and contemporary way to meet other mums and create the community she so urgently needed. And so, in 2017, Peanut was born, an app that allows women to connect with other women who are at a similar stage in life – from fertility, pregnancy and motherhood through to menopause. My goodness, Peanut was a lifeline for me in the days when I was early on in my pregnancy, and I hadn't told many people and wanted to feel less alone. Then later in the pandemic, the app brought a whole new meaning to community for me; at a time when we couldn't actively go out and meet people, the power of Peanut became unmissable. Michelle has an impressive CV. Before Peanut, she was the Deputy CEO of Badoo and one of the first board members of Bumble. Michelle and I spoke about her experience of growing a company and family as well as the importance of women having a seat at the table.

Reflecting on my experience of navigating my career and having a family, my experience has been different with both of my children. When I started Peanut, Finlay was two and a half. He was just starting to go to nursery in the mornings, and we were starting to get into more of a routine. He and I really knew each other and he just came along with it.

If I was going to the States, he was coming to the States with me; if I was going to speak at an event on a weekend, he was coming with me. He really just folded into it all, because so much of what I was building with Peanut was so close to his life and what I'd experienced with him in my life as a parent. So building Peanut felt very very connected to my journey as a parent and working mum.

As the business grew and his life grew, it became less possible to take him along with me. He has his own life. He has clubs, he has his own little world which isn't about me. It became much harder to bundle him up and fit his life neatly into mine. You also get to the point where you are missing stuff. I'm not going to be the person who picks him up from his first week at school. I might drop him off, but I'm not going to pick him up. Or there's a choice to be made between going to Ruggerbugs with him or a commitment for the business. Choices like this I had to make and that became hard as he grew and the business grew.

When I was pregnant with Nula, it was a whole different landscape. I was fundraising for the company, and I had a very difficult pregnancy. I was very sick, and I was growing the team and growing the business. So that was hard. I found the pregnancy really difficult; I'd be on the way to investor meetings and I would ask the cab driver to pull over so I could throw up. Looking back, I made some decisions throughout that pregnancy that, in hindsight, I'm not very proud of and I wouldn't make again.

There was a day when I hadn't felt her move for a while, and I went to the investor meeting rather than going to the hospital first as a priority. Obviously I then didn't perform in the investor meeting, because I was obsessively thinking about the fact that I hadn't felt her move. So there were things like that, where I didn't get my priorities right. You're right; I think there really is no balance – it's just a complete myth. It's about everything coming together. It's also important to learn that it's okay to prioritise what you need and not always what you think should be the priority – such as the business or work.

With Nula, I feel a lot of guilt. I couldn't just bundle her up and taken her on the journey like Finlay, largely because of lockdown. I definitely got more facetime with her, but running a business in lockdown means that you are sitting at your screen all day on video calls. *The other day she thought that our CTO lived in my computer, because she's only ever seen him on my screen. So it's challenging that she's grown up with a lot of screens in her life, and with us not being able to necessarily detach work from family life, and her not being able to be a part of the excitement of the journey of building the business.*

So where Finlay has a real attachment to what I've done because he's been involved in so much of it, Nula hasn't had that same exposure. Now I have a team of thirty-five people, and it's much harder to bring her into my office because we're at a different stage now. So the experience of motherhood and running a business, which is not just a business but a start-up, into growth is challenging, laced with guilt and laced with rethinking my priorities a lot. But certainly, the further in I get, and also with age, I get a bit more cantankerous and I have a clear idea of what I will and won't accept. I don't accept that someone puts a meeting in my diary at seven o'clock. Because that's bedtime, and I want to put my kids to bed. I don't accept that. IF my kids appear in a video call now and again, people have to deal with it, because that's life these days. And so I have become a little bit less afraid of owning motherhood in what I do. Which is ironic because, notwithstanding the nature of the business that I built for so long, the motherhood part of my life felt like it had to be put in a corner. So it's complicated, but I think it's getting better.

I'm really passionate about women and working mums taking up senior positions and rightfully having a seat at the table.

We were never, ever told what the impact of family life would be on us when we were told we could be anything. We're of the era where we were told you can be as good as a man and you can be at the top, and, yes, we know of the glass ceiling that exists that makes it harder for us, but family life was never really factored into that.

On top of that, from a societal perspective, we do nothing to help women: we don't have affordable childcare; we don't have all the necessary infrastructure in place. It's very easy to start to look at the whole infrastructure and how it's set up and the challenges that one can face and think, Well, it's just not for me. But the challenge with that is, if we've been told that we can be anything and we should be anything, then there's a huge responsibility that comes with that, in terms of the women who are coming behind us. That includes our children or our nieces or whomever. There is a real need for us to show up and take on these roles at the 'top', because the consequence of not taking the leap and not taking the risk is that people turn around and say, 'I told you so, you didn't deserve that place, or you can't handle it.'

We can't afford to lose the ground that we've gained; look at what is happening in the US with Roe v. Wade. It's starting to undermine how far we've come. We can't contribute to that narrative by saying, 'Oh, but you know, it's not really right for me.' The reality is that it's scary and the infrastructure is not where it should be; it's not adequately set up. But if we don't jump, it won't get better. And so I definitely think, as women, we just figure things out. For example, men have always been given the benefit of the doubt; that they'll figure it out. Yet because we've been schooled to not take risks and to feel like we must have a plan and have everything structured, we don't really take the leap. I truly believe you can figure it out by having a community of people around you, the right support network, asking for help and not expecting to do it all on your own. It is not a solo game; it's a multiplayer game. Men don't do it all on their own – they have their networks, they rely on referrals – and yet so many women try to make it on their own.

Be your own best hype woman!

As I forensically examine the stories of many successful working mums, there are quite a few things that jump out at me. One of those things is that they are not afraid to express their desire to progress and reach new heights. In fact, they are unapologetically vocal about their abilities, achievements and ambitions. In many ways, it takes heaps of confidence and self-belief, but somewhere along the line, I think it's also been ingrained in us as women not to celebrate our achievements, not to show up for ourselves, and that to get ahead we have to lay low or be humble. I've seen it in lots of returning mums battling with their own self-belief and have been guilty of it myself. There is nothing wrong with humility – it very much serves an important purpose in the right context – but it can be a hindrance when it prevents us from stepping into potential opportunities.

Often, visible ambition is confused with aggression or treading on other people's toes, and therefore it can be aligned with not being liked. And it's that fear of not being liked that can really have a huge impact on how we express ourselves. As a result, so many of us hold ourselves back or don't take the credit for something we have worked hard for, because we're afraid of being perceived as pushy, braggy or too ambitious. The problem is that if we don't advocate for ourselves, how can anyone else accurately advocate for us in rooms where career-altering decisions are being made? The same goes for waiting for opportunities to be handed to us. Sometimes, we have to put ourselves out there and ask for the opportunities, even if it feels a bit uncomfortable. But we shouldn't be afraid to work on our confidence continuously to help us connect with and go for the right opportunities.

I am a work in progress in this area, but one of the things that has helped me is having a group of friends that genuinely champion one another. Some of us are mums, but the common unifying factor is that we all have huge dreams, and we consistently support each other and hold each other accountable as we work hard towards them. It's the power of sisterhood. In fact, some of these special women feature in the book, and they have been incredible sources of encouragement to me. Gosh, on so many occasions we've swapped messages, helped each other out in job negotiations or difficult conversations at work, or just been a shoulder to cry on when things get tough. We call each other out when we think that someone is selling themselves short or holding themselves back from a huge opportunity. I must give credit where credit is due, and say my husband has also been instrumental in helping me find my confidence. So, having the support of like-minded, trusted people can really help on your journey of self-confidence and vocalising your ambitions.

If you could do just one practical thing as a result of reading this book, then let it be this: Practise finding your voice. You can start with the small things like reviewing your achievements, writing them down and focusing on what you did that brought about a positive result. I know in my speech, I find it so easy to say 'we' instead of 'I'; 'we' just rolls off the tongue so naturally. But I have found it really helpful to write down in my personal document of achievements when I have personally made something happen. I promise you that if you try this over and over again when it comes to moments like performance reviews, it becomes much easier to express your own achievements. Some people find affirmations helpful, and so you may want to try that too. For example I often repeat affirmations like, 'I have all the skills to do an incredible job. I am more than capable and I am destined for greatness.'

I hope that you are inspired to continue to believe in yourself, share your accolades and go after opportunities that you want with both hands.

Build your village

Another common denominator of successful working mums is that they have a village of people around them to help. I used to think that being a successful mum was about doing everything myself, making fresh meals from scratch and keeping the house immaculate. I quickly discovered that it was impossible to do those things at the same time as building the future I wanted for my family; plus, I wasn't a huge fan of making baby food from scratch. It was hard to let go at first and allow others to step in, because I feared I would be less of a mother for doing so or that people would judge me. Yet in the stories that India, Holly, Laura and Michelle have shared, they all have a structure that allows them to perform at work and fulfil their responsibilities at home. Even if they may not be the ones actually doing all the tasks at home, it doesn't matter – the tasks are still getting done, which frees them up to be there for the important moments in their children's lives. If you are raising a child with your partner, please, please, please make sure that you discuss how responsibilities will be shared. I would even advise that if you know that you want kids and are heading into a relationship where kids look like they are on the cards in the future, have this conversation about potential responsibilities early on. Talk about your ambitions and what kind of village you want to build to help you achieve the goals that you have for yourself and your future family. Keep the conversation going, because ambitions and responsibilities will change over time.

There are lots of brilliant businesses being created to help give busy parents more time. For example, Mamamade is a business that delivers fresh homemade baby meals to your door, the Bubble app is brilliant for babysitting, and Koru Kids can help with finding ad hoc and longer-term childcare. My village consists of a roster of different people and services. My family are the foundation of my village, and when they are not available I have a combination of a local nanny, a babysitter from Bubble and one of the staff from my kids' nursery whom I can call upon. I know that my neighbours and school mums would happily help out too, if I ever got stuck somewhere.

No one should be made to feel guilty for creating the right structures to help them at work and at home. Having the right structures in place is an extremely positive thing if it works well for you. It's super important to mention that a robust village may sound like an expensive solution, if straight away your mind goes to a nanny and a housekeeper. I would love a housekeeper, but the reality is that it won't be possible financially. So, if possible, ask family, friends or neighbours to chip in now and again to start with. Your village does not need to be paid help. It can be colleagues or mentors to provide support to you and your career. It can be local community groups where your child has an opportunity to play and you can build local relationships. As your career grows and progresses, you may want to think about factoring the cost of your village into your cost of living when discussing your salary.

What does success mean to you?

Finding your way to the top means very different things to everyone. For some people, it is about a role in the C-suite; for some, it's about building a business; for others, it's about leading on pioneering research or amassing the kudos and the accolades needed to be able to choose what they want to do and how they spend their time. It could also be all or none of the above. It's important to define what success means to you. Remember to also find joy on your journey as you work towards your goals. Reflect on your journey often and celebrate key milestones. What success means to you can also change, and that is more than okay. At thirteen I wrote down twenty or so goals for myself, and when I look back on them, now I laugh. Some of those goals have happened and some I haven't even come close to achieving, because my idea of what success is has changed dramatically with age and again with motherhood.

It is also okay to not have it all figured out, and the majority of us haven't. I asked the My Bump Pay community what success means to them and I just had to share some of the answers with you, as I thought they were so honest and thought-provoking. And if you are still on the journey to fleshing out what success means to you, then I thought these may be helpful as a source of inspiration. They may also be helpful to you in working out what success *isn't*.

Here is what some people had to share about what success is to them:

- *being confident in my role at work*
- *not comparing myself to others*
- *being content with the decisions I've made in life and not being overwhelmed by the 'what ifs' and things that could have been*
- *being debt-free, with a good amount of savings and a thriving marriage*
- *surviving the day with work and a toddler*
- *seizing opportunities with both hands and making the very best of them*
- *a job that I truly love*
- *I deeply value living and thriving, especially after the death of a close friend*
- *a decent salary, financial freedom and healthy work–life blend*
- *making a positive and lasting impact on the lives of others*
- *money*
- *staying committed to my goals*

You might be reading this thinking that your definition of success isn't just one thing, it's a combination of different factors. Refreshingly, it's true that long-lasting success is made up of different components. Research by Laura Nash and Howard H. Stevenson uncovered four clear components of enduring success:[34]

1. Happiness (feelings of contentment regarding one's life);
2. Achievement (accomplishing the things that you have

strived for); 3. Significance (the feeling that you have made a positive impact on those closest to you); 4. Legacy (a way to use your successes and learn to help others to find their own success in the future).

It's also okay for success to mean different things at different times. For you, success in the early years of your little ones' lives may be about prioritising family, and your other goals may have to be reprioritised for a season. Or you may decide that you want to focus on both at the same time and build the right support around you to make it happen.

Finding your own personal definition of success will help you to stay focused, block out the naysayers and the distractions, and motivate you on the hard days. We all have one shot at life, and the journey of motherhood should never stop you from giving it a go, shooting for the stars and leaving your 'what ifs' behind.

Being a mum is your superpower

The journey to motherhood and motherhood itself will build a strength in you that you never realised you had, and that strength is your superpower. I truly believe that motherhood actually makes many of us better leaders in the workplace, and therefore we are the perfect candidates to be smashing the glass ceiling. We appreciate the value of time now that we have competing responsibilities, and often cut through the noise to focus on getting things done. We multitask better, we have more empathy, and we have no choice but to build the skills of prioritisation. A 2018 study of working Americans showed that 91% believe working mums bring unique skills to leadership roles, and 89% feel they bring out the best in employees.[35] The same study also revealed some other powerful facts: 84% of those surveyed believe that having mothers in leadership roles will make a business more successful; 65% of participants describe working mums as better listeners than other employees; and 51% describe mothers as calmer in a crisis. You are innately qualified to lead and rise to the top as you make your way through this motherhood journey.

In many ways, it is hard to write closing words or statements, because the conversation isn't done yet. We are just scratching the surface of showing everyone what mums or those who wish to be mums can achieve and contribute to our world. I'm so, so, so excited to see more stories of more incredible women rising through the ranks with a family in tow. So much so that I'd love to read your own personal stories of you finding your own success and smashing the glass ceiling with a baby on the way and beyond. So please do email me at Stories@mybumppay.com and let's celebrate the trailblazing stories that deserve to be recognised.

I've always said that everything I do on this mission is about impact, and so I hope that the words in this book can impact as many people as possible. And as you soar, why not look behind you, reach out your hand and impact the life of another woman at the start of her journey.

Acknowledgements

I truly believe it takes a village to raise a mother and a child, and through this experience I have humbly learned that it takes a village to raise an author. So, to my incredible village, I want to say a huge thank you for supporting me through thick and thin; without you, none of this would be possible.

I would like to say how deeply grateful I am to my wonderful publisher, Anna, for having faith in me and believing that I could share this collection of stories to help make a wide impact on as many people as possible. I also couldn't have embarked on this journey without my agent, Julia Silk! Thank you for support, clarity and words of wisdom throughout this process.

A special thank you to all the amazing contributors: thank you for your time and vulnerability, and for allowing me to share your stories so honestly. Every single one of you is such an inspiration to me. I'm so proud to know you all and to watch the beauty of your journeys unfold.

Mum and Dad, words will never quite be enough to express just the depth of my love and respect for you both. Everything that I've ever achieved is because of your sacrifice, hard work and love. Thank you for the foundation of self-belief that you've instilled in me, thank you for teaching me the value of hard work, and thank you for supporting me to boldly live out my dreams.

To my husband, I know you hate the spotlight, but you deserve a shining mention. You more than anyone have seen all the beautiful chapters of this journey. Thank you for being my rock, a compassionate listening ear and my fiercest cheerleader. Thank you for being an incredible father to our beautiful children, and thank you for giving me the time and space to write this book.

Dr Tosin! The best sister a girl could ask for! Thank you for being one call away whenever we need an extra pair of hands, a second opinion and a good laugh. No matter how busy your schedule is, you always make the time for us and the kids absolutely adore you. Thank you for being such an inspiration, and for being a formidable part of our village.

Notes

Introduction

1. Post, Corrine, Lokshin, Boris, and Boon, Christophe (2021). 'Research: Adding Women to the C-Suite Changes How Companies Think'. *Harvard Business Review*. Available at: https://hbr.org.2021/04/research-adding-women-to-the-c-suite-changes-how-companies-think

2. 'Families and the Labour Market, UK: 2019'. *Office of National Statistics*. Available at: https://www.ons.gov.uk/employmentandlabourmarket/peopleinwork/employmentandemployeetypes/articles/familiesandthelabourmarketengland/2019

3. McGinn, Kathleen L. and Lingo, Elizabeth Long (2015). 'Mums the Word! Cross-national Effects of Maternal Employment on Gender Inequalities at Work and at Home'. *Harvard Business School*. Available at: https://hbswk.hbs.edu/item/mums-the-word-cross-national-effects-of-maternal-employment-on-gender-inequalities-at-work-and-at-home

Chapter 1

4. Henrik, Kleven, Landais, Camille and Egholt Søgaard, Jakob (2019). 'Children and Gender Inequality: Evidence from Denmark.' *American Economic Journal: Applied Economics*, 11(4): 181–209.

5. Leung, M. Y. M., Groes, F. and Santaeulalia-Llopis, R. (2016). 'The Relationship between Age at First Birth and Mother's Lifetime Earnings: Evidence from Danish Data'. *PLOS ONE*, 11(1): e0146989. https://doi.org/10.1371/journal.pone.0146989

6. Hirsch, Donald (2020). 'The Cost Of A Child In 2020'. *Child Poverty Action Group*. Available at: https://cpag.org.uk/sites/default/files/files/policypost/CostofaChild 2020_web.pdf

7. NHS (2020). 'Infertility'. Available at: https://www.nhs.uk/conditions/infertility/

8. Tommy's (2020). 'Baby Loss Statistics'. Available at: https://www.tommys.org/baby-loss-support/pregnancy-loss-statistics

9. Payne, Nicky and van den Akker, Olga (2016). 'Fertility Network UK Survey on the Impact of Fertility Problems'. *Fertility Network*. Available at: https://fertilitynetworkuk.org/wp-content/uploads/2016/10/SURVEY-RESULTS-Impact-of-Fertility-Problems.pdf

Chapter 2

10. Topping, Alexandra (2021). 'How do UK childcare costs stack up against the best?' *Guardian*. Available at: https://www.theguardian.com/moey/2021/sep/12/

how-do-uk-childcare-costs-stack-up-against-the-best

11. Hamilton, Rosie (2022). 'Help with Childcare Costs'. *MoneySavingExpert*. Available at: https://www.money savingexpert.com/family/childcare-costs/

12. Prospect (2021). 'What is the gender pay gap?' *Prospect*. Available at: https://prospect.org.uk/article/what-is-the-gender-pension-gap/

Chapter 4

13. Hideg, I., Krstic, A., Trau, R. N. C. and Zarina, T. (2018). 'The unintended consequences of maternity leaves: How agency interventions mitigate the negative effects of longer legislated maternity leaves.' *Journal of Applied Psychology*, 103(10): 1155–1165.

Chapter 7

14. HSE (2021). 'Protecting pregnant workers and new mothers.' *Health and Safety Executive*. Available at: https://www.hse.gov.uk/mothers/employer/rest-breastfeeding-atwork.htm

15. Foust-Cummings, Heather and Dinolfo, Sarah (2011). 'Sponsoring Women to Success.' *Catalyst*. Available at: https://www.catalyst.org/research/sponsoring-women-to-success/

16. Kelliher, C. and Anderson, D. (2010). 'Doing more with less? Flexible working practices and the intensification of work.' *Human Relations*, 63(1): 83–106.

17. Department for Business Innovation and Skills.

18. ACAS (2021). 'New study reveals half of employers expect more flexible working requests from staff after the pandemic is over.' Available at: https://www.acas.org.uk/new-study-reveals-half-of-employers-expect-more-flexible-working-after-pandemic
19. GOV.UK (2021). 'Making flexible working the default.' Available at: https://www.gov.uk/government/consultations/making-flexible-working-the-default
20. Van Bommel, T. (2021). 'The power of empathy in times of crisis and beyond.' *Catalyst.* Available at: https://www.catalyst.org/reports/empathy-work-strategy-crisis

Chapter 8

21. van Scheppingen, M. A., Dennisen, J. J. A., Chung, J. M., Tambs, K. and Bleidorn, W. (2017). 'Self-Esteem and Relationship Satisfaction during the Transition to Motherhood.' *Journal of Personality and Social Psychology,* 114(6), 973–991. Available at: https://doi.org/10.1037/pspp0000156
22. Vodafone. (2021). 'Lost Connections: Supporting returners into the workplace in 2021 and beyond – a WPI Strategy Report for Vodafone'. Available at: https://newscentre.vodafone.co.uk/app/uploads/2021/05/Lost-Connections-2021-180521-Pages-Web-1-1.pdf
23. Slepian, M. L., Ferber, S. N., Gold, J. M. and Rutchick, A. M. (2016). 'The Cognitive Consequence of Formal Clothing.' *Social Psychological and Personality Science,* 6(6): 661–668.

Chapter 9

24. United Nations (2016). 'Women's economic empowerment in the changing world of work,' Report of the Secretary-General. *Economic and Social Council.* Available at: https://www.un.org/ga/search/view_doc. asp?symbol=E/CN.6/2017/3

Chapter 10

25. McKinsey and Company (2019). 'Diversity wins: How inclusion matters.' Available at: https://www.mckinsey. com/featured-insights/diversity-and-inclusion/diversity-wins-how-inclusion-matters.pdf
26. Landais, C., Dias, M. C., Bandiera, O. and Andrew, A. (2021). 'The careers and time use of mothers and fathers.' *The Institute for Fiscal Studies* (IFS Briefing Note; No. 319). Available at: https://doi.org/10.1920/BN. IFS.2021.BN0319
27. McKinsey and Company (2016). 'The Power of Parity: Advancing Women's Equality in the United States.' Available at: https://www.mckinsey.com/featured-insights/employment-and-growth/the-power-of-parity-advancing-womens-equality-in-the-united-states
28. Fawcett Society, Sex Equality: State of the Nation, 2016.
29. McGinn, Kathleen L. and Lingo, Elizabeth Long (2015). 'Mums the Word! Cross-national Effects of Maternal Employment on Gender inequalities at Work and at Home.' Harvard Business School Working Knowledge.

30. McKinsey and Company and LeanIn.Org. (2019). 'Women in the workplace.' Available at: https://www.mckinsey.com/featured-insights/diversity-and-inclusion/women-in-the-workplace
31. Foust-Cummings, Heather and Dinolfo, Sarah (2011). 'Sponsoring Women to Success.' *Catalyst*. Available at: https://www.catalyst.org/research/sponsoring-women-to-success/
32. Sieghart, Mary Ann. *The Authority Gap*. (London: Transworld, 2019).
33. McKinsey and Company (2021). 'A fresh look at paternity leave: Why the benefits extend beyond the personal. Available at: https://www.mckinsey.com/business-functions/people-and-organizational-performance/our-insights/a-fresh-look-at-paternity-leave-why-the-benefits-extend-beyond-the-personal

Chapter 11

34. Nash, Laura and Stevenson, Howard H. (2004). 'Success that lasts.' *Harvard Business Review*. Available at: https://hbr.org/2004/02/success-that-lasts
35. Bright Horizons (2018). 'Modern Family Index 2018.' Available at: https://www.brighthorizons.com/-/media/bh-new/newsroom/media-kit/mfi_2018_report_final.ashx

Resources

Author resources

My Bump Pay Resources: https://mybumppay.com/resources/

Employee helplines

Pregnant Then Screwed helpline: 0161 222 9879
ACAS: 0300 123 1100

Baby loss

Beyond Grief: Navigating the Journey of Pregnancy and Baby Loss by Pippa Vosper

Careers

The Squiggly Career: Ditch the Ladder, Discover Opportunity, Design your Career by Helen Tupper and Sarah Ellis

Entrepreneurship

Do What You Love, Love What You Do by Holly Tucker

Money

Five Steps to Financial Wellbeing by Clare Seal

Love is Not Enough: A Smart Woman's Guide to Money by Merryn Somerset Webb

Smart Women Finish Rich by David Bach

Confidence

Know Your Worth: How to Build Your Self-Esteem, Grow in Confidence and Worry Less about what People Think by Anna Mathur

Success

'Success That Lasts' by Laura Nash and Howard H. Stevenson: https://hbr.org/2004/02/success-that-lasts

Paternity leave

'A Fresh Look at Paternity Leave: why the benefits extend beyond the personal': https://www.mckinsey.com/business-functions/people-and-organizational-performance/our-insights/a-fresh-look-at-paternity-leave-why-the-benefits-extend-beyond-the-personal

Parenting

What's My Child Thinking? Practical Child Psychology for Modern Parents by Tanith Carey

Women in the workplace

'The careers and time use of mothers and fathers', Alison Andrew, Oriana Bandiera, Monica Costa Dias Camille Landais, *The Institute for Fiscal Studies* (2021)

'The Power of Parity', McKinsey (2016): https://www.mckinsey. com/~/media/McKinsey/Featured%20Insights/Gender%20 Equality/Women%20in%20the%20Workplace%202019/Women-in-the-workplace-2019.ashx

'Women in the Workplace 2019', McKinsey and Lean In.

'Diversity Wins: How Inclusion Matters', McKinsey (2019): https:// www.mckinsey.com/featured-insights/diversity-and-inclusion/ diversity-wins-how-inclusion-matters.pdf

My Life in Full: Work, Family, and Our Future by Indra Nooyi

The Authority Gap by Mary Ann Sieghart

Index

adoption 40–41

age
  decision to start a family 13–14
  fertility treatment 31

Ajaja, Deborah 100–103

allies at work 283–292

ambition
  case studies 297–308
  importance of 293–294
  personal success 313–315
  self-advocacy 308–310, 311

annual leave 56–57, 93

antenatal appointments 89

appointments
  antenatal 89
  fertility treatment 32

Asare, Tobi
  background 5–7, 75–77,
    147–148
  childcare 256–257
  decision to start a family 12,
    15–16
  first pregnancy 44–45, 77–78,
    161–162
  life as a working mum
    247–249
  life insurance 267
  maternity leave 107–108,
    124, 224, 228–229
  My Bump Pay development
    7–9, 43, 147, 151, 157
  parents 75–76

return to work 181–183
second pregnancy 78
assumptions about working
    mothers 285–286
authority gap 287
automation of business
    processes 140–141
availability, setting boundaries
    253

baby equipment
    essentials cost 46–47
    nearly new shopping 47
baby loss 23–30, 37–39, 135,
    147, 272–273
bias about working mothers
    285–286
blend, the
    career progression 259–263
    challenges 274–282
    concept 249–250
    having more children
        263–274
    setting boundaries 251–259
boundary setting 251–259, 302
Brady, Karen 294
Brearley, Joeli 276
breastfeeding 187, 190

business, benefits of women in
    leadership roles 4, 283–284
    .
career breaks and pensions 73
career goals
    aligning with organisational
        goals 94, 96, 196, 203–204
    impact of maternity leave
        length 112–113
    maternity leave 128–131
    mentors and sponsors 97–99,
        101, 192–195, 197, 287–288
    networking 96–97
    planning and listing 14–15,
        265–266
    return to work 191–197
    skill gaps 105–106
    success, personal meaning
        313–315
    see also promotions; visibility
career performance
    documenting 99–100, 114,
        205, 207, 214, 226–228,
        310
    feedback 261–262
    fertility treatment 32
    pregnancy 84–85
    promotions 260

securing a sponsor 98, 101
career progression, company
    measurement 292
cars 65
cashback sites 57
Channel 4 26
charities, baby loss 30
Chen, Eva 208
Child Benefit 64
childcare
  back-up options 176
  childminders 169–170
  commuting considerations
    163–164
  costs 60–64, 163–164, 264
  deciding on 163, 175–176,
    178–179, 265
  deposits 61
  effect on mortgages 65
  'floating hours' 145
  grandparents 173–174
  having more children 264,
    265
  investment attitude 66–67,
    200
  nannies 170–173
  nurseries 165–168, 177
  partners 256

planning in advance 86–87,
    104
return to work 184
shift work 189
work pattern considerations
    165
childminders 169–170
children, having routines
    149–150
clients expectations, maternity
    leave 139–140
clothing and confidence
    233–238
Coleridge Cole, Georgie 143–146
community building 150–151
commuting
  childcare 164
  while pregnant 85–86
company policies
  baby loss 26–27, 38
  employment termination
    218
  feedback and review 290
  fertility treatment 32–33
  flexible working 218
  maternity 18–19
conceiving and changing jobs
    20–23

confidence
    clothing 233–238
    definition 223–224
    maternity leave 105, 225–232
    mum guilt 238–243, 251–
        252, 276
    return to work 183–184,
        223
    self expectations 244–245,
        269–270, 278
    self-advocacy 308–310
    side hustles 157–158
    visualisation 232, 242
Corbett-Winder, Sarah 237
costs see money
critical illness cover 70

dads see partners
deadlines, setting boundaries
    254–255
delegation 255
discrimination
    maternity leave 112–113
    mothers 263, 276–277
    paternity leave 291
    pregnancy 82–83, 95, 98–99,
        126, 276–277

email, planning for maternity
    leave 92–93
emotions
    having more children 266–
        267
    money 67–68
    return to work 181–183
empathy 216, 272, 290, 316
equal opportunities 4, 194, 269,
    283–284
Ettus, Samantha 257
expectations, realistic 244–245,
    269–270, 278

feedback 261–262, 290
Fenton, Laura 300–303
fertility treatment 30–37, 146
finance see money
Fiverr 155
flexible working 93, 104–105,
    146, 209–212, 218
focus 184–185, 302
founders
    planning for maternity leave
        139–143
    side hustles 147–159
    statutory maternity pay
        135–136

freelancers *see* self-employment
friends *see* support network

Garfinkle, Adam 261
Gary Martin, India 260, 297–300
glass ceiling 3–4, 285, 307
grandparents, childcare 173–174
grants: Sure Start 57
guilt 238–243, 251–252, 276, 295–296, 299, 305

help, asking for 206–207
home working
    clothing 235–236
    return to work 205–207
    while pregnant 85
house moves 65, 177

imposter syndrome 244
    see also confidence
infertility 23–24
    see also fertility treatment
intentionality 15–16, 94, 202–203
interviews 220–221
IVF *see* fertility treatment

jobs
    changing after maternity leave 215–222
    changing while pregnant 269–270
    changing while trying to conceive 20–23
    company benefits for parents 92, 217
    effect of maternity leave lengths 110
    interviews 220–222
    see also career-related entries

Kennedy, Michelle 303–308
KIT days (keeping in touch) 90–91, 92, 113, 189–190, 228–229

leadership roles
    balance 271
    empathy 216, 272, 290
    infrastructure for career progression 307–308
    positive impact of women 4, 283, 315–316
    sponsors 287–288
legislation for baby loss 25–26, 38

Liddell, Maia 178–179
life insurance 65, 70
LinkedIn 97, 209, 220, 229,
    268–273

marketing for side-hustles
    154–155
MAT B1 form 50, 87–88
maternity cover
    handover 88, 89, 91, 114,
        141
    planning 80, 86, 139–143
maternity leave
    annual leave 56–57
    checklist 91–93
    communicating plans with
        managers 125–126
    communications during 115
    confidence 225–231
    impact of other paid leave
        policies 19
    KIT days (keeping in touch)
        90–91, 92, 113
    length 109–113, 124
    mindset 126–131, 259–260
    planning 88–91
    see also shared parental leave
        (SPL)

maternity pay
    bonuses 54–55
    budgeting 55, 65, 72, 124,
        142–143
    documentation 50, 87–88
    emotions 67–68
    enhanced maternity pay
        52–54
    founders 136
    knowing company policy
        18–19, 71, 93, 264–265
    maternity allowance 51–52,
        134–136
    statutory 48–50, 135–136
Mathur, Anna 243–245,
    258–259, 267
mentors 97–98, 192, 193,
    195
mindset for maternity leave
    126–131, 259–260
miscarriage 25–28, 38, 147
mistakes, making 231–232
money
    budget for maternity pay 55,
        65, 72, 124, 142–143
    cashback sites 57
    childcare costs 163–164,
        167–168

cost of baby's first year
43–47, 72, 73–74
cost of raising a child 19
emotions 67–68
having more children
264–265
hidden costs 65
investments for children
69–70, 73
personal financial security
69–71
plans for starting a family
18–20
salary negotiation 200
savings 56, 72, 142–143
side-hustle budgeting
153–155
Sure Start grant 57
see also maternity pay
Morrison, Illy 267
mortgages 65
motherhood
superpower 315–316
and work 199–200, 283–286
mum guilt 238–243, 251–252,
276, 295–296, 299, 305
My Bump Pay 7–9, 43, 124,
147, 150, 151, 157, 229–230

nannies 170–173
Nash, Laura 314–315
National Insurance, credits
from Child Benefit 64, 66
networking
job changes 219–220
during maternity leave 131
during pregnancy 96–97, 105
return to work 208–209
side hustles 152–153
nurseries 165–168, 177

Ogunkoya, Yewande 279–282
O'Leary, Cara 268–273
opportunity costs 156–157
organisation 185–186
out-of-office responses 92–93
outsourcing 155–156, 158–159,
186, 256–257

parental leave, shared (SPL)
58–60, 71–72, 115–123,
291–292
partners
baby loss 28–29
childcare 256
discussions on starting a
family 17–18, 311

flexible working 104
paternity leave and pay 58,
    291–292
pay gap statistics 13, 284–285
Peleton 150–151
pensions
    career breaks 73
    Child Benefit credits 64, 66
    nannies 172
    pension gap 65–66
perception, by others 261–262
perfection 156, 231–232
performance at work *see* career
    performance
performance reviews 93,
    130–131, 218
positivity on return to work
    114
pregnancy
    first trimester 83–86
    risk assessments at work 95
    second trimester 86–88
    telling work 77–83, 146
    third trimester 88–93
prenatal courses 87
process automation 140–141
productivity with flexible
    working 212

profile, in career progression
    262–263
promotions
    3Ps 260–263
    after return to work 259–263
    while on maternity leave
        106
    while pregnant 100–103
purpose, identifying 248

Rabadia, Jaz 33–37
receipts exercise 226–228,
    241–242
resilience 220–221
return to work
    after baby loss 27
    breastfeeding 187, 190
    career goals 191–197
    childcare 184
    confidence 183–184, 223, 232
    emotions 181–183
    flexible working 209–212
    focus 184–185
    management support
        288–290
    mum guilt 239
    networking 208–209
    new roles 110–111

organisation 185–186

phased 187

planning before maternity
leave 89–90, 103–106

planning on maternity leave
188–189

positivity 114

reviews 197

with a side-hustle 158–159

support network 212–213

visibility 201–207

risk assessments 95

Robb, Nishma 198–199

routines

children 149–150

return to work 186

salary negotiation 200

savings 56, 72

schools, planning ahead 68–69,
177

Seal, Clare 71–74

self-belief 157–158

see also confidence

self-care

after baby loss 28

importance of 257–259,
275–276

maternity leave 127–128

mum guilt 239–240, 242–243

in third trimester 88–89

self-employment

baby loss 39

financial planning 135–136

maternity allowance 51–52,
134–136

side hustles 147–159

Shabaya, Sagina 21–23

shared parental leave (SPL)
58–60, 71–72, 115–123,
291–292

shift work 189, 190

sickness

childcare 168, 171, 172, 256

pregnancy-related 77, 78,
85–86

side hustles 147–159

Sieghart, Mary Ann 287

skill gaps 105–106

social events at work 95, 96

socialising 65

sponsors 97–99, 101, 192–195,
197, 287–288

stakeholders, communication
with 86, 88, 92, 114, 197,
204–205

starting a family
    financial plans 18–20
    partner discussions 17–18,
        311
    timing 12–17
statutory maternity pay 48–50,
    136
statutory paternity pay 58
Stedman, Alexandra 136–139
Stevenson, Howard H. 314–315
stillbirth 25–28, 38
success, personal meaning
    313–315
succession plans 139–140
superpower of motherhood
    315–316
superwoman complex 274–275,
    278, 298, 307
support network
    career goals 298–300, 308,
        309–310
    company organised 217
    confidence 230–231
    discussing starting a family
        17–18, 311
    fertility treatment 33
    maternity leave 128
    other mums 87

return to work 212–213
small business start ups
    152–153
tough times 278–279
village building 87, 298,
    311–312
at work after baby loss 28,
    29–30
Sure Start grant 57

tax, self-employment and
    founders 142
tax-free childcare 61–63, 264
therapy after baby loss 28
time as opportunity cost
    156–157
Tomlinson, Davina 69–71
training during maternity leave
    229–230
    see also KIT days (keeping in
        touch)
Tucker, Holly 294–297

Universal Credit, childcare help
    63

Vandermolen, Brooke 188–
    191

video calls / meetings 27,
    205–206, 305–306
village building 87, 298,
    311–312
virtual assistants (VAs) 155–156
visibility
    during maternity leave 90,
        129–130
    during pregnancy 95–96

profile 262–263
return to work 201–207
visualisation 232, 242
Vosper, Pippa 37–40

wills 70–71
working hours, UK statistics
    4–5
work-life balance *see* blend, the